The US Congress

Anthony J. Bennett

Advanced
Topic*Master*

Series editor
Eric Magee

Philip Allan Updates, part of the Hodder Education Group, an Hachette Livre UK company, Market Place, Deddington, Oxfordshire OX15 0SE

Orders

Bookpoint Ltd, 130 Milton Park, Abingdon, Oxfordshire OX14 4SB
tel: 01235 827720
fax: 01235 400454
e-mail: uk.orders@bookpoint.co.uk
Lines are open 9.00 a.m.–5.00 p.m., Monday to Saturday, with a 24-hour message answering service. You can also order through the Philip Allan Updates website: www.philipallan.co.uk

© Philip Allan Updates 2007

ISBN 978-1-84489-444-4

First printed 2007
Impression number 5 4 3 2 1
Year 2012 2011 2010 2009 2008 2007

Printed in Spain

Environmental information
Philip Allan Updates' policy is to use papers that are natural, renewable and recyclable products and made from wood grown in sustainable forests. The logging and manufacturing processes are expected to conform to the environmental regulations of the country of origin.

P01072

Contents

Introduction

Confusions and paradoxes about Congress

Back in the days immediately after the Second World War, before the outbreak of the Cold War, a Russian named Boris Marshalov was taken into the public gallery in Congress to watch the debates of the House of the Senate. Marshalov was not a great devotee of democracy and presumably had little experience of legislative debate. Upon leaving Capitol Hill, he was asked by a friend what he thought of Congress in session. 'Congress is so strange,' he is reputed to have replied. 'A man gets up to speak and says nothing — and then everybody disagrees.' Some would wish to suggest that little has changed in Congress in the last six decades.

But Americans' views of and reactions to Congress seem confusingly mixed and are enshrined in this paradox — that although most Americans hold Congress as an institution in low esteem, they seem to hold their own members of Congress in very high esteem, and continually re-elect them at election after election. Presidents who have an approval rating in the 30–40% range will find it well nigh impossible to get re-elected. Ask Jimmy Carter or the first George Bush. But while Congress's approval rating regularly languishes in these regions — and even lower — re-election rates for the House are consistently in the high 90% range, and are only marginally lower in the Senate. The rule seems to be that unless you have committed some evident faux pas — either political or ethical — you are pretty much a shoo-in for re-election as a member of Congress.

Americans are also somewhat unsure as to what is the correct balance between presidential power and congressional power. Do they want the president to provide leadership and the Congress merely to rubber-stamp White House activity, or do they fear an over-powerful president and look to Congress to use its checks and balances with ruthless efficiency? When things go wrong — politically, economically, socially or internationally — do ordinary Americans blame the president or Congress? Which institution is held most responsible?

There is another paradox about Congress — that although ordinary Americans are quite frequently in touch with their Senators and House member, they probably know little — and understand even less — about the way Congress works and what Congress actually does. Media coverage of the presidency is more

likely to come on a day-to-day basis than coverage of Congress. Television news coverage of congressional business tends to play second fiddle to the daily White House press briefing. Americans can even learn about how the presidency works from watching *The West Wing*. No one has yet come up with a television series based in Congress. Only the true politics wonks will sit down and watch C-SPAN — the cable station offering gavel-to-gavel coverage of the House and the Senate — on anything like a regular basis, if at all.

Neither does the language or procedure of Congress help much. Switch on C-SPAN or sit in the House or Senate galleries and you will be bombarded with talk of 'adjournments', 'authorisations', 'calendars', 'entitlements', 'motions to proceed', 'non-germane amendments', 'quorum calls', 'reconciliations', 'riders', 'supplemental appropriations' and questions as to whether this or that person will 'yield the floor' or 'yield time'. It's a foreign language to all but committed congressional devotees.

Even in academic circles, for every book published on Congress there seem to be at least two dozen (if not more) published on the presidency. Information on Congress is not so easy to find. This book hopes to fill something of a gap for those beginning a serious study of US government and politics.

The questions to be answered

The aim of this book is to discuss six key questions about the US Congress. The first is: *How representative is Congress?* This takes us back to theories of representation and asks questions about how representative Congress is in terms of gender and race, as well as analysing how and to what extent members of Congress represent their constituents. Does it matter whether or not Congress 'looks like America'? Are members of Congress truly representatives or merely delegates?

We then move on to the workings of Congress and specifically to how Congress passes legislation. The second question is: *Why is it so hard to pass legislation through Congress?* During the 109th Congress (2005–06), of the 13,072 bills that were introduced, a mere 395 (3%) were passed into law. We shall examine the political and structural reasons why this was the case, as well as look at a case study of the 2001 'No Child Left Behind' Act, which was George W. Bush's legislation for education reform.

As long ago as 1885, Woodrow Wilson — later to become US president — stated that 'Congress in session is Congress on public exhibition, whilst Congress in its committee rooms is Congress at work'. What was true of Congress towards the end of the nineteenth century is no less true now at the beginning of the twenty-first century. Our third question therefore is: *Why are congressional committees so important?* We shall discover that the answer is tied up with the fact that congressional standing committees are permanent, policy specialist institutions, which play a strategic role both in legislation and in overseeing the executive branch. Unlike their UK parliamentary counterparts, they offer a significant career path for legislators, one that would interest many far more than a post in the executive branch of government.

Conventional wisdom suggests that Congress has become a body that is more ideologically divided than was the case two or three decades ago. If this conventional wisdom is correct, what are reasons behind this change? Our fourth question is: *Why has Congress become more partisan?* We shall discover that the conservative Democrat and the moderate Republican in Congress are both becoming something of an endangered species. What are the effects of this and does it matter?

At the start of the 110th Congress in January 2007, 50 members of the Senate had previously served as members of the House of Representatives. This figure was actually down by 2 on that for the 109th Congress. But why do so many House members seek to get elected to the Senate while none move in the reverse direction? Our fifth question is: *Better to be a Senator than a House member?* We shall discuss issues such as career paths, terms of office, representation and exclusive powers to discover the answer.

Finally, we shall ask: *What's wrong with Congress?* At a time when approval ratings for Congress seem to be at an all-time low, this is a pertinent question. A lack of competitive House seats, the growth of ideological polarisation, abuse of the Senate filibuster and ineffective oversight of the executive, as well as other internal structural weaknesses, will all point to there being some significant things wrong with Congress.

To allow you to extend your research, further reading lists are given at the end of most chapters. Useful websites are as follows:

www.house.gov

www.c-span.org

www.politics1.com

http://thomas.loc.gov

www.senate.gov

www.loc.gov

www.washingtonpost.com

How representative is Congress?

Theories of representation

Before we can discover how representative Congress is, we must be clear what it means to be 'representative'. The subject of representation in a democracy is complicated because, like the term 'democratic', it has many different meanings. Unless one were living in a 'direct democracy' — a system of government in which political decisions are made by the people directly rather than by elected representatives — the concept of representation is important and difficult to address. But direct democracy has never been used widely in the United States, though we get near to it in some states' use of referendums and 'initiatives'. Direct democracy is really only practical in small communities and to resolve simple issues of policy.

Theories of representation fall into two main categories: representation to mean 'acting for', and representation to mean 'standing for'. In the first category, we are concerned with the *how* of representation; in the second, we are concerned with the *who*. When considering representation in terms of 'acting for', there is a further dilemma: should elected officials represent the *national* interest, as for example Edmund Burke argued, or should they reflect the interests of a locality, as James Madison recommended.

'Acting for'

Indeed, the question of how the people should be represented is as old as the theory of democracy itself, and many of the great political theorists have written about it. In what is often called the *reactionary theory of representation*, expounded by such people as Thomas Hobbes and, in America, Alexander Hamilton, the need for order and authority is paramount. Public officials — either in the executive (preferably a monarch) or legislative branches — serve the public interest as they perceive it. While they might be open to some input from the citizenry at large, these public officials — being of superior judgement and knowledge — should not feel particularly checked by the popular will. The people for their part are expected to support the state and to accept the policies enacted by the government. This is an elitist position, and some would even argue that it is undemocratic and indeed not really 'representative' at all.

A less extreme position was taken by such political philosophers as Edmund Burke, John Stuart Mill and James Madison. They proposed the conservative theory of representation, in which the people choose those who are to govern them from an elite group. There is no sense in which the people 'instruct' their elected representatives or that they can in any way compel them to reflect the popular will on a given issue. If, however, the representatives do not act in a way that satisfies the people, then the people may replace them with others at the next election. This is also referred to as the *trustee model of representation*.

Then there is the liberal theory of representation, expounded by people such as John Locke and Thomas Jefferson. This theory is based on the concept of equality. Whereas the reactionary and conservative theories of representation are elitist, the liberal theory of representation is pluralist. If all are equal, then all are equally capable of ruling and making decisions. In this theory, the elected representative acts as a kind of messenger for his or her constituents rather than as a policy maker per se. This is also referred to as the *delegate model of representation*.

There is too what might be called a party theory of representation. This is particularly relevant in those nation states that have strong, centralised, disciplined and ideologically distinct political parties. In this theory, the political parties put their policies before the people in manifestos at a general election. In electing a government, the people are thereby endorsing the manifesto of the winning party, which can claim a mandate to carry out all those policies in the period between taking office and the next general election. Hence this is also referred to as the *mandate model of representation*.

Put more simply, in the trustee model it is the politician's views that are important. In the delegate model, it is the people's views that are important. In the mandate model, it is the party's views that are important.

'Standing for'

There is another sense in which we can use the term 'representation', which we are calling the 'standing for' theory of representation. This is not concerned with *how* the people are represented, but *who* represents them. It is often referred to as the *resemblance model of representation*: to what extent representatives

'resemble' (or look like) those whom they are representing. The usual categories with which 'resemblance' is concerned are gender, race, age, profession, religion and geographic region. In the UK one would probably add social class, but not in the United States.

Now that we know what representation means, we can examine the question of 'how representative is Congress?' in these different ways. We shall begin with the issue of resemblance as it will thereby enable us to study who is doing the representing before considering how they do it.

Congress and gender

The facts

Congress has for most of its history been seen as a men's club. It was not until the passage of the 19th Amendment (1920) that American women were guaranteed the vote in elections for Congress. The first woman was elected to Congress 4 years before that — Jeanette Rankin, a Republican from Montana elected to the House of Representatives in the elections of 1916. Since then, a further 209 women have been elected to the House from the 50 states. The state-by-state breakdown is shown in Table 1.1. Only six states have failed to elect a woman to the House of Representatives — Alaska, Delaware, Iowa, Mississippi, North Dakota and Vermont. When Mary Fallin was elected to the House as a Republican in 2006, she was the first woman elected to the House from Oklahoma since 1920.

Table 1.1 Women in the House of Representatives by state, 1916–2007

State	Number of women elected to the House since 1916	Democrats	Republicans
California	29	23	6
New York	20	13	7
Illinois	12	4	8
Florida	10	6	4
Ohio	8	4	4
Maryland	7	4	3
Michigan	7	5	2
Washington	7	3	4

State	Number of women elected to the House since 1916	Democrats	Republicans
Connecticut	6	4	2
Pennsylvania	6	5	1
Georgia	5	5	0
Indiana	5	4	1
Missouri	5	4	1
New Jersey	5	2	3
South Carolina	5	5	0
Tennessee	5	2	3
Texas	5	4	1
Arkansas	4	4	0
Hawaii	4	2	2
Kansas	4	3	1
North Carolina	4	2	2
Oregon	4	4	0
Colorado	3	2	1
Massachusetts	3	1	2
Minnesota	3	2	1
Utah	3	2	1
Virginia	3	1	2
Arizona	3	3	0
Idaho	2	1	1
Kentucky	2	0	2
Louisiana	2	2	0
Maine	2	0	2
Nevada	2	1	1
New Mexico	2	1	1
Oklahoma	2	1	1
West Virginia	2	1	1
Wisconsin	2	2	0
Alabama	1	1	0
Montana	1	0	1
Nebraska	1	0	1
New Hampshire	1	1	0
Rhode Island	1	0	1
South Dakota	1	1	0
Wyoming	1	0	1

Of the 210 women who have served in the House of Representatives, 36 were elected to fill vacancies caused by the death of their husband. Fifteen of that 36 were subsequently elected to serve additional terms. The longest serving woman in the House was Edith Rogers, a Republican from Massachusetts who served for 35 years. Seven of these 210 women went on to be elected to the Senate. The youngest woman to serve in the House was Elizabeth Holtzman, a Democrat from New York, who was elected in 1972 at the age of 31.

The first woman to serve in the Senate was 87-year-old Rebecca Felton, a Democrat from Georgia. She was appointed in 1922 but served only 1 day! Altogether, 35 women have served in the Senate, of whom 13 were first appointed and 5 were elected to fill an unexpired term. This includes Lisa Murkowski of Alaska, who was appointed to the 108th Congress to fill the vacancy caused by the resignation of her father, Frank Murkowski, and then elected in 2004 to a full 6-year term in her own right.

Table 1.2 Number of women in Congress, 1979–2007

Years	Congress	Number of women in House	Number of women in Senate	Total number of women in Congress
1979–80	96th	16	1	17
1981–82	97th	21	2	23
1983–84	98th	22	2	24
1985–86	99th	23	2	25
1987–88	100th	23	2	25
1989–90	101st	29	2	31
1991–92	102nd	28	4	32
1993–94	103rd	47	7	54
1995–96	104th	48	9	57
1997–98	105th	54	9	63
1999–2000	106th	56	9	65
2001–02	107th	59	13	72
2003–04	108th	60	14	74
2005–06	109th	67	14	81
2007–08	110th	71	16	87

Three states — California, Maine and Washington — are currently represented in the Senate by two women: Barbara Boxer and Dianne Feinstein, both Democrats, represent California; Susan Collins and Olympia Snowe, both Republicans, represent Maine; and Patty Murray and Maria Cantwell, both Democrats, represent Washington State. For a brief period in 1996, Kansas was represented by two Republican women Senators, Nancy Kassebaum and Sheila Frahm, the latter appointed to fill the vacancy caused by the resignation of Bob Dole. The youngest woman elected to the Senate is Blanche Lincoln of Arkansas. She was elected in 1998 at the age of 38 and is currently in her second term.

As recently as 1979–80 (the 96th Congress), of the 535 members there were only 17 women in Congress (16 in the House; 1 in the Senate). This figure had grown to 87 by January 2007 (the 110th Congress), with the significant increase coming in 1992, which the Democrats had dubbed 'the year of the woman' in an effort to get women candidates into winnable seats. In January 1993, the number of women in the House rose from 28 to 47, and in the Senate it was up from 4 to 7. But increases in subsequent elections have been much smaller. By the 110th Congress (2007–08) women constituted just 16% of the US Senate and 16% of the House.

The reasons

These facts raise the obvious question: 'Why are there so few women in Congress?' There are two rather obvious and connected reasons: first, there are few women in the pools of recruitment from which members of Congress are drawn; and second, few women candidates are chosen. Let us consider each in turn.

Table 1.3 **Previous elective office held by women members of the US House of Representatives, 110th Congress (2007–08)**

Previous elective office held by women members of US House	Total
State representative	32
State Senator	16
Council member	13
County governing board member	10
Judge	5
School board member	3
State-wide elective office	3
Mayor	2

Source: Center for American Women and Politics website (www.cawp.rutgers.edu)

Of the 71 women members in the House of Representatives at the start of the 110th Congress (January 2007), 53 (74.6%) had previously held elective office and 28 of that 53 had held more than one elective office prior to reaching the US House of Representatives. As Table 1.3 shows, the most common pool of recruitment for women members of the House is from the lower houses of the state legislatures, from which 32 had come. But not only are women under-represented in the US Congress, they are also under-represented in state legis-latures. In 2007, of the 7,382 state legislators across the 50 states, only 1,734 (or 23.5%) were women.

Of the 16 women members of the Senate at the start of the 110th Congress, 11 had held previous elective office and 8 of that 11 had held more than one elective office prior to reaching the Senate. As Table 1.4 shows, the two most common pools of recruitment for women Senators are the lower houses of state legislatures and the US House of Representatives. And we already know that both these pools contain few women.

Table 1.4 **Previous elective office held by women members of the US Senate, 110th Congress (2007–08)**

Previous elective office held by women members of US Senate	Total
State representative	7
US House of Representatives	6
State Senator	3
County governing board member	2
State treasurer	2
Mayor	1
Council member	1
City board of supervisors	1

Source: Center for American Women and Politics website (www.cawp.rutgers.edu)

It is therefore reasonable to conclude that one of the prerequisites for increased representation of women in the US Congress is the increase of female representation in state legislatures. But, as Table 1.5 shows, there is little evidence that this is occurring. Indeed, the increases there of late have been even slower than at the federal level. Since 1979, while women's representation in Congress has increased five-fold, their representation in state legislatures has only increased just over two-fold. State legislatures experienced no similar boost in women's membership as a result of the Democrats' 'year of the woman' in 1992.

Table 1.5 Women's membership of US Congress and state legislatures compared, 1979–2007

Year	Percentage of women in US Congress	Percentage of women in state legislatures
1979	3	10
1981	4	12
1983	4	13
1985	5	15
1987	5	16
1989	5	17
1991	6	18
1993	10.1	20.5
1995	10.3	20.6
1997	11.0	21.6
1999	12.1	22.4
2001	13.6	22.4
2003	13.6	22.4
2005	15.0	22.6
2007	16.3	23.5

Source: Center for American Women and Politics (www.cawp.rutgers.edu)

This leads us to our second reason — that few women are chosen as major party candidates in congressional elections. Indeed, the share of women candidates has increased at a slower rate than the share of women members in the period since the 1978 election. Whereas women members in the House have increased more than four-fold (from 16 to 67) between the 1978 and 2006 elections, Table 1.6 shows that the number of women candidates for House seats increased only three-fold (from 46 to 136). In the Senate, 2006 saw a record number of women candidates — 12 — but this bettered the 1984 figure by only 2.

It was to reverse these trends that the pressure group EMILY's List was formed in 1985. Its aim is the election of pro-choice Democratic women to federal, state and local office. It seeks to do this through 'recruiting strong candidates, training campaign staff and making sure that [women candidates] have the resources to win.' EMILY is not a person but an acronym for Early Money Is Like Yeast. Just as in baking bread, where yeast in the dough helps it to rise, so early money is thought to be crucial in the success of a challenger's political campaign. You can find out more information at the website www.emilyslist.org.

Table 1.6	Number of women candidates for House and Senate seats, 1978–2006	

Year	Women candidates for House seats	Women candidates for Senate seats
1978	46	2
1980	52	5
1982	55	3
1984	65	10
1986	64	6
1988	59	2
1990	69	8
1992	106	11
1994	112	9
1996	120	9
1998	121	10
2000	122	6
2002	124	11
2004	141	10
2006	136	12

Source: Center for American Women and Politics (www.cawp.rutgers.edu)

The implications

So women are consistently under-represented in Congress. But does it matter? In her research for the Center for American Women and Politics, entitled *Representing Women: Congresswomen's Perceptions of their Representational Roles*, Susan Carroll reached the conclusion that 'women representatives are more likely than their male colleagues to support feminist positions on so-called "women's issues", to actively promote legislation to improve women's status in society, and to focus their legislative attention on issues such as healthcare, the welfare of the family, and education.'

An analysis of the way women members of Congress play their representative role raises the issue of what is called 'surrogate representation'. Surrogate representation occurs when a member of Congress represents the interests of voters beyond the boundary of their own state or district. In this sense, women members of Congress would see themselves as not only representing their own constituents, but also those women who live outside their state or district. This is how Republican Senator Olympia Snowe of Maine sees surrogate representation:

Because we represent half the population, I have always felt the special concern and the unique responsibility to single out those issues that are so important and critical to the future of women because their voices cannot be heard otherwise. It's not that male colleagues don't represent those issues; as a general population, they do. But I think that women in Congress will give special attention to those issues. We tend to carve them out as priorities, and that is important because so often women have been overlooked as a priority in some of the issues.

And here's Democrat Senator Barbara Boxer of California:

There are still so few women in Congress. So really you have to represent more than your own state. But women from all over the country really do follow what you do and rely on you to speak for them on issues of women's healthcare, reproductive choice, condition of families, domestic priorities, environment, and equal pay for equal work. It's a pretty big burden.

There is, of course, no direct accountability for this form of representation. Olympia Snowe and Barbara Boxer are only accountable to the voters of Maine and California respectively.

However, while the majority of women members of Congress think and act as surrogate representatives for American women as a whole, it would be misleading to think of women House and Senate members as a uniform voting bloc. They differ quite markedly in the districts they represent, their ideological perspectives and their partisan commitments. For example, Senators Barbara Boxer of California and Kay Bailey Hutchison of Texas don't vote together very often. Senator Boxer is a liberal Democrat while Senator Hutchison is a relatively conservative Republican.

Within Congress there is actually a bipartisan group called the Congressional Caucus for Women's Issues, which tries to devise a collective strategy on issues of special interest to women. Examples of legislation that the women's caucus has successfully supported are the creation of federal protections against domestic violence and sexual harassment. But with the election of more conservative Republican women into Congress, we have also seen the women's caucus backing legislation to outlaw gay marriage and promote such pro-life policies as the ban on late-term abortions.

More recently, women have increased their impact in Congress by taking up leadership positions in both chambers. At the start of the 110th Congress in 2007, the Speaker of the House of Representatives was for the first time a woman — Nancy Pelosi of California — and two Senate standing committees were chaired by women — Environment and Public Works by Barbara Boxer and Rules and Administration by Dianne Feinstein, both from California. In the House, Louise Slaughter of New York became chair of the prestigious House Rules Committee.

Congress and race

The facts

The second most important way we should look at Congress in terms of the resemblance model of representation is race — specifically as regards African-Americans and Hispanics, by far the largest two racial minority groups in the United States.

Table 1.7 **States with more than 10% African-American population (2000 census)**

State	Percentage African-American (2000)
Maryland	21.45
Georgia	17.68
South Carolina	16.68
Mississippi	15.71
Louisiana	15.33
North Carolina	13.76
Virginia	13.57
Alabama	13.51
Delaware	12.66
New York	12.19
New Jersey	11.11

The 2000 census showed that African-Americans made up 12.3% of the American population. But as Tables 1.7 and 1.8 show, this varies significantly from state to state. Washington DC is 58% African-American.

Since the end of the Civil War there have been 101 African-American members of Congress — 96 in the House and just 5 in the Senate. Of this 101, 22 served in the Reconstruction Era between 1869 and 1901 and all were Republicans. Abraham Lincoln's Republican Party had fought against slavery in the Civil War and hence blacks voted for and joined 'the party of Lincoln'. There were no African-American members of Congress between 1901 and 1929. Of the 74 African-Americans in Congress in the modern (post-1929) era, all but 4 have been Democrats. The last African-American Republican to serve in the Senate was Edward Brooke of Massachusetts (1967–79) and in the House it was J. C. Watts of Oklahoma (1995–2003).

Table 1.8 **States with less than 1% African-American population (2000 census)**

State	Percentage African-American (2000)
Montana	0.16
Vermont	0.27
South Dakota	0.27
Maine	0.29
North Dakota	0.32
Idaho	0.43
Utah	0.54
New Hampshire	0.54
Wyoming	0.65
Iowa	0.88
Oregon	0.96

Table 1.9 **States returning the most African-American members of Congress, 1929–2007**

State	Number of African-American members of Congress since 1929	Rank in percentage of African-American population (2000)
Illinois	15	12th
California	10	22nd
New York	9	10th
Michigan	5	14th
Texas	5	15th
Georgia	5	2nd
Maryland	4	1st
Pennsylvania	4	21st

The states that have returned the most African-American members of Congress since 1929 are shown in Table 1.9. The only state in the *bottom half* of the ranking of African-American population in the 2000 census which has ever returned an African-American member of Congress is Massachusetts (28th). Similarly, there are only three states in the *top half* of those same rankings which have never returned an African-American member of Congress — Delaware (9th), Arkansas (16th) and Kentucky (24th). Thus it is clear that the return of American-American members to Congress is linked to their representation within the population of the various states.

Figure 1.1 **Distribution of African-Americans in the United States (2000 census)**

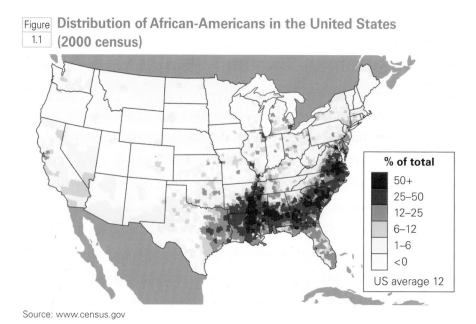

Source: www.census.gov

The reasons

Since the 1940s, no state has had a majority African-American population, making it increasingly difficult for an African-American candidate to be elected solely by the black vote. But despite this, three African-Americans have won state-wide races for the US Senate during this period — Edward Brooke in Massachusetts (1966) and Carol Moseley Braun (1992) and Barack Obama (2004), both in Illinois.

Following the 1990 census, a number of states redrew their congressional district boundaries — those boundaries used for electing House members — so that the majority of the population would be African-Americans. These were so-called 'majority-minority districts'. As a direct result of this, the number of African-Americans in the House increased in the 1992 congressional elections — the first elections to be held with the newly drawn districts — from 26 to 38, a significant rise. The states that used such majority-minority districts

Barack Obama, one of three African-Americans to have won state-wide races for the US Senate since the 1960s

were Alabama, California, Florida, Georgia, Louisiana, Maryland, North and South Carolina, Texas and Virginia. In four of these states, the result was the first African-American elected to Congress since Reconstruction: in South Carolina the first since 1896, in Virginia the first since 1890, and in both Alabama and Florida the first since 1874. This brought African-American representation in the House to 9%, only slightly below the national representation of 12%.

But as Burdett Loomis (*The Contemporary Congress*, 2004) points out:

> In recent years, some scholars have challenged the effectiveness of majority-minority districts both in terms of producing policies that are favourable to minorities and sending more minority representatives to the House. If the purpose of the majority-minority districts is to elect more minority members of Congress, the current system can be counter-productive by marginalising the electoral prospects of minority candidates.

Take North Carolina, for example, which has 13 congressional districts. The two majority-minority districts — the 1st and the 12th — each return an African-American House member by huge margins. In 2004, Melvin Watt won the 12th District with 67% of the vote and a 33% margin over his Republican challenger. But the two neighbouring districts — the 5th and 6th — now have such a tiny percentage of black voters — 7% and 8% respectively — as to almost completely silence the voice of black interests.

Of the 37 African-American House members at the start of the 109th Congress (2005), 27 of them represented districts in which African-Americans were the largest single racial group. Only one district in which African-Americans made up less than a quarter of the population returned a black House member — Emanuel Cleaver in Missouri's 5th District, where African-Americans make up 24.2% of the population.

With so few House seats likely to return an African-American candidate, there are frustratingly few opportunities for black politicians to seek federal office. Black politicians also have some of the safest seats, making vacancies unlikely. When an opportunity does appear, there is often a crowded field of would-be African-American House members. When Democrat Kweisi Mfume of Maryland resigned from the House in 1996 to head the NAACP, 32 people filed for the Democratic primary in a congressional district that has almost 60% black voters.

The implications

The Congressional Black Caucus has become known as a bastion of left-orientated Democrats in Congress — and all its members are Democrats. That gives the caucus much more unity than the women's caucus. Examples of policy areas which the Black Caucus has pioneered include social welfare policy and issues concerning urban renewal.

In roll-call votes, African-American House members are even more liberal than their Democrat colleagues. Each year the liberal pressure group Americans for Democratic Action (ADA) rates each member of Congress according to the percentage of major votes he/she casts in agreement with the ADA's position. In the 107th Congress (2001–03), Democrat House members as a whole averaged a 77% rating, while African-American Democrats averaged 88%.

African-American members of Congress can also have an impact as role models in government. According to political scientist Michael Preston, 'blacks need representatives that they believe will represent their interests; they need to know that leadership is not dominated by one race or group.'

Like women, African-American legislators see themselves as exercising some degree of surrogate representation. But this is less pronounced than it is for women, as so many African-Americans live within districts represented by African-Americans. Indeed, this has become more the case with the introduction of majority-minority districts.

It is also true that African-American members of Congress are significantly disadvantaged in a period of Republican dominance because they are currently associated exclusively with the Democratic Party. As a result they held no leadership positions in either chamber between 1995 and 2007. However, with Democrats regaining control of both chambers in 2007, John Conyers — the founding member of the Congressional Black Caucus — became Chair of the House Judiciary Committee, and Charles Rangel succeeded to the chair of the prestigious House Ways and Means Committee. Furthermore, James Clyburn of South Carolina was elected House Minority Whip, the third most senior post in the House of Representatives.

Hispanics in Congress

The 2000 census showed that Hispanics made up 12.5% of the American population, thus becoming the largest single minority and overtaking African-Americans for the first time. The term 'Hispanic' includes people of different races. The 2000 census showed that the Hispanic community was 58.5% Mexican, 9.6% Puerto Rican, 4.8% Central American (including El Salvador and Guatemala), 3.8% South American (including Columbia and Ecuador), 3.5% Cuban, 2.2% from the Dominican Republic, and 0.3% Spanish. People of other Hispanic origin made up the remaining 17.3%.

Hispanic power at the ballot box is still much less significant than that of African-Americans, for three reasons. First, the Hispanic community is a young community. At the 2004 election, only 41% of Hispanics had reached the voting age, compared with 76% for whites and 65% for blacks. Second, Hispanics of voting age are less likely than other Americans to be registered voters. This is partly due to a language barrier. And third, even when registered, Hispanics eligible to vote are less likely to turn out. Only 45% of eligible Hispanics voted in the 2000 election compared with 61% of other eligible adults.

Table 1.10 **States with more than 10% Hispanic population (2000 census)**

State	Percentage Hispanic (2000)
New Mexico	42.1
California	32.4
Texas	32.0
Arizona	25.3
Nevada	19.7
Colorado	17.1
Florida	16.6
Illinois	12.3

Table 1.11 **Hispanic members of Congress by state (2007)**

State	Number of Hispanic members of Congress
California	7
Texas	6
Florida	4*
Arizona	2
Colorado	2*
New York	2
New Jersey	2*
Illinois	1

*Includes one Senator.

There is no doubt that Hispanics will become increasingly important in future decades. Six of the 8 states where Hispanics make up more than 10% of the population (see Table 1.10) have growing populations and hence more representation in the House. Between them these 8 states added 8 more seats in the House of Representatives in 2002 as a result of the post-2000 census redistricting. In comparison, the 11 states in Table 1.7 (states in which African-Americans make up more than 10% of the population) gained no extra seats after redistricting.

There are currently 23 Hispanic members of the House of Representatives. This means that Hispanics form just under 6% of the House membership. In terms

of party allegiance, 20 are Democrats and 3 are Republicans. There are currently 3 Hispanic Senators — Ken Salazar (Democrat) of Colorado, Robert Menendez (Democrat) of New Jersey and Mel Martinez (Republican) of Florida, all of whom came into the Senate since 2004. The Congressional Hispanic Caucus (CHC) was formed in 1976 and states its aims as 'addressing national and international issues and the impact these policies have on the Hispanic community'. Its membership is exclusively Democrat. The Congressional Hispanic Conference was formed in March 2003 by Mario Diaz-Balart (Republican–Florida). Its stated aims were to 'support President Bush and American troops in the war against terrorism, the Free Trade Agreement of the Americas, tax relief to families and over 2 million Hispanic and Portuguese owned small businesses, support for faith-based initiatives, and educational choice for all', altogether a very different platform from the CHC. Its membership is exclusively Republican.

Figure 1.2 **Distribution of Hispanics in the United States (2000 census)**

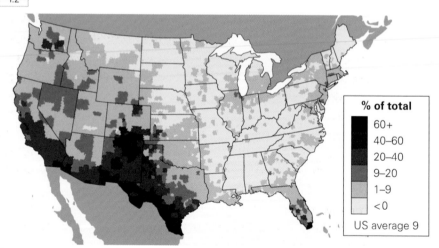

Source: www.census.gov

Because the longest-serving Hispanic members of Congress are Democrats, they were — like their African-American counterparts — disadvantaged by the continued Republican control of Congress between 1995 and 2007. With the Democrats recapturing control of the House in 2007, Solomon Ortiz of Texas became chair of the House Armed Services Subcommittee on Readiness. Hispanics' 6% of House membership and 3% of Senate membership is well below their 12.5% national population. But this may change as the Hispanic community grows and ages, thus entering those other pools of recruitment from which members of Congress are drawn.

Other representational factors

We have considered gender and race in some detail as important representational factors. If Congress is to fit the resemblance model of representation, its members need to 'look like America', to use Bill Clinton's phrase for his planned cabinet after the 1992 election. In terms of gender, Congress clearly looks nothing like America at all. In terms of race, representation is marginally better, especially in the House of Representatives.

In terms of **age**, Congress is decidedly elderly. At the start of the 110th Congress (2007), the average age of the House was 56, and the Senate came in at just under 62. There were only 25 House members — and no Senators — under the age of 40.

In terms of **education**, Congress is highly educated. In the Senate, 78 members have advanced degrees — meaning a masters or doctoral degree — as do 280 of the 435 House members. Lawyers make up 58% of the Senate and over one third of the House.

In terms of **religion**, Congress is quite representative, at least as regards the various branches of the Christian churches. Roman Catholics predominate, followed by Baptists and Episcopalians (what we would call Anglicans). Jews are well represented in Congress — there are 26 in the House and 11 in the Senate. The first Muslim was elected to Congress in November 2006 — Keith Ellison (Democrat), elected to the House from the 5th District of Minnesota.

As regards **geographic region**, the Founding Fathers determined that the two chambers of Congress would be used to represent different interests. Disagreement at the Philadelphia Convention as to whether the states should be equally represented in Congress or be represented in proportion to population led to the compromise of the Senate's membership being equal for all states while the membership of the House is proportional to each state's population. Hence the Senate was to represent the interests of the small-population states, while the House was to represent those of the large-population states.

Thus, in the Senate, the 26 smallest-population states that could command a majority of the votes on the floor — 52 of the 100 — represent a mere 17% of the American population. Indeed, the combined population of those 26 states — just over 50 million — is less than the combined population of California and Texas, which is over 54 million. However, in the House of Representatives the combined voting strength of those 26 smallest-population states is just 76 votes, whereas the combined voting strength of California and Texas is 85 votes. This shows clearly the different basis of representation in the two houses of Congress.

Representing constituents

We now turn to that other facet of representation — the way and the extent to which members of Congress represent the views of their constituents. It is generally thought that members of the House place a higher premium on this function than do Senators. There are three reasons for this. First, they serve much shorter — 2-year — terms compared with the 6-year terms of Senators. Second, many states add a 'locality rule' — that House members must reside in the district they represent — to the constitutional requirement to reside merely in the state they represent. Third, most House districts are far more homogenous constituencies than those which Senators represent.

Take Loretta Sanchez, a Democrat representing the 47th District of California. Sanchez is one of the 23 Hispanic House members. Her district, in the heart of Orange County, covers just 55 square miles. Its population of 640,000 is 65% Hispanic and 100% urban. Consider the rather more straightforward task she may have in representing her constituents than do either of the California Senators, fellow Democrats Dianne Feinstein or Barbara Boxer. They must each represent 34 million Californians spread across 164,000 square miles — an area nearly twice the size of the UK. And their voters are not homogenous at all — they are 47% white, 32% Hispanic, as well as 11% Asian.

The methods

Members of Congress have a number of ways to try to represent their constituents. On the floor of the chamber they can fulfil this function through making speeches and voting. In committee, they can seek assignment to committees and subcommittees that are of particular relevance to their constituents. In their offices — whether in Washington or back in their state or district — they can provide a whole range of constituent services.

In his book *How Congress Works and Why You Should Care* (Indiana University Press, 2004), former House member Lee Hamilton, who represented Indiana's 9th district from 1965 to 1999, tells the following anecdote:

> One evening I was walking out of the Capitol with Wilbur Mills, an enormously powerful legislator from Arkansas who had long chaired the House Ways and Means Committee. His picture had even been on the cover of *Time* magazine and he was known all over the country for his power over the US tax code and his role in setting up Medicare. Powerful people sought his advice and clamoured to speak with him even for a few seconds. I asked him where he was going and he said, 'I'm going back to Arkansas. I'm holding a public meeting.' He mentioned some small Arkansas town and said, 'There'll be about fifteen or twenty people there.' As we parted he said, 'Lee, don't ever forget your constituents. Nothing, nothing comes before them.' I never forgot it.

To illustrate the link between members of Congress and their constituents, let's take two of the current members of the Kansas state delegation in the House. Jerry Moran, a Republican, represents the First District, a huge, sprawling area of nearly 60,000 square miles of prairie that is two-thirds the size of the UK. The district is 48% rural. He grew up in Plainville, Kansas, a tiny town of around 2,500 people, in the district he now represents. He then worked locally as a banker before attending the University of Kansas Law School, gaining a bachelor's degree in 1970. After spending time as lawyer, he was elected to the state Senate in 1988 and to Congress in 1996. Moran is a member of the House Agriculture Committee, where he is 4th out of 21 in Republican seniority. He is on two of the subcommittees — General Farm Commodities and Risk Management, where he is the Ranking Minority Member, and Conservation, Credit, Rural Development and Research. He also serves on the Transportation and Veterans' Affairs committees. Military veterans make up 13.4% of his constituents.

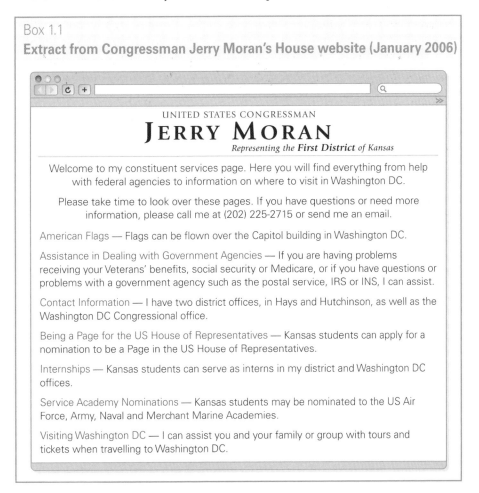

Box 1.1

Extract from Congressman Jerry Moran's House website (January 2006)

UNITED STATES CONGRESSMAN

JERRY MORAN

*Representing the **First District** of Kansas*

Welcome to my constituent services page. Here you will find everything from help with federal agencies to information on where to visit in Washington DC.

Please take time to look over these pages. If you have questions or need more information, please call me at (202) 225-2715 or send me an email.

American Flags — Flags can be flown over the Capitol building in Washington DC.

Assistance in Dealing with Government Agencies — If you are having problems receiving your Veterans' benefits, social security or Medicare, or if you have questions or problems with a government agency such as the postal service, IRS or INS, I can assist.

Contact Information — I have two district offices, in Hays and Hutchinson, as well as the Washington DC Congressional office.

Being a Page for the US House of Representatives — Kansas students can apply for a nomination to be a Page in the US House of Representatives.

Internships — Kansas students can serve as interns in my district and Washington DC offices.

Service Academy Nominations — Kansas students may be nominated to the US Air Force, Army, Naval and Merchant Marine Academies.

Visiting Washington DC — I can assist you and your family or group with tours and tickets when travelling to Washington DC.

Dennis Moore, a Democrat, represents the Third District. It's just 787 square miles, is mostly made up of Kansas City and is 95% urban. He grew up in Wichita, Kansas. He went to college and law school in Kansas before being elected as a district attorney in Johnson County, which is within the district he now represents. He was first elected to the House in 1998. Moore is a member of the House Budget Committee where he is now number 20 out of 22 in Democrat seniority. He also serves on the Financial Services Committee. Both congressmen have constituency service pages on their House websites, extracts from which you can see in Boxes 1.1 and 1.2.

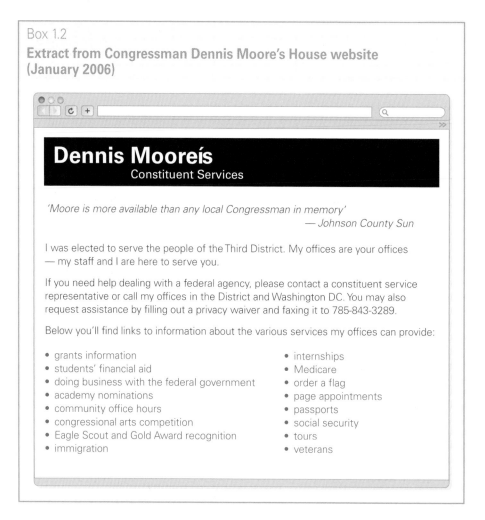

Box 1.2

Extract from Congressman Dennis Moore's House website (January 2006)

Dennis Mooreís
Constituent Services

'Moore is more available than any local Congressman in memory'
— Johnson County Sun

I was elected to serve the people of the Third District. My offices are your offices — my staff and I are here to serve you.

If you need help dealing with a federal agency, please contact a constituent service representative or call my offices in the District and Washington DC. You may also request assistance by filling out a privacy waiver and faxing it to 785-843-3289.

Below you'll find links to information about the various services my offices can provide:

- grants information
- students' financial aid
- doing business with the federal government
- academy nominations
- community office hours
- congressional arts competition
- Eagle Scout and Gold Award recognition
- immigration

- internships
- Medicare
- order a flag
- page appointments
- passports
- social security
- tours
- veterans

By 2004, Sheryl Wooley had served as chief of staff to Republican Congressman Porter Goss of Florida for 15 years. In an interview that year, she talked about the way Goss served his constituents of southwest Florida:

Constituents' problems are varied. Residents of a town want the town to have its own postal address to stop mail being diverted — and often either delayed or lost — through a nearby larger city. Another group wants Interstate 41 [the main north–south transport link through western Florida] widened. Then there are concerns over the protection of the Florida Everglades, which form part of the eastern portion of the district. And given the position of the district [a coastal district in southwest Florida] immigration issues are common. In addition there are tax issues, healthcare or Medicare problems and the non-arrival of Social Security cheques. The office typically receives 300–400 e-mails a week on top of the more traditional letters and phone calls which still arrive at the rate of around 1,000 per week when Congress is in session and around 500 per week during congressional recess periods.

This, along with frequent visits back to the state or district — depending on distance — will help to keep the member of Congress in tune with what constituents think and want. Back home, there will be a constant round of meetings — Town Hall [i.e. public] meetings, party meetings, meetings with business people, teachers, healthcare professionals, law enforcement officers, the local media, voluntary groups, as well as meetings at schools, hospitals, local chambers of commerce or Round Table events. And there are also the one-on-one meetings with constituents to fit in too.

Representation through voting

Both chambers offer ample opportunity for casting votes — mostly on legislation and budget matters. During 2006, there were 543 recorded votes in the House and 279 in the Senate.

To what extent do members of Congress consider the views of constituents when voting? The answer is quite complicated. First, it will vary from one member to another. Second, even for one member it will vary from vote to vote. Some issues will have a clear constituency interest while others will not. Third, it depends on what other influences are being brought to bear on a particular vote — from the party, interest groups or the administration, for example.

But one must remember that it is more difficult than it first appears to actually discern what the views of constituents are on a given issue. For all the e-mails and letters read, the phone calls answered, the meetings attended, and the questions answered, what the member of Congress is reading and hearing may merely be what one sceptical House member described as 'what folks don't like from the folks who don't like it'.

In an interview just before his nomination as CIA Director in 2004, Republican Congressman Porter Goss had this to say about voting in Congress:

> When it comes to votes on the House floor, I'm very supportive of the Bush White House and of the House Republican leadership. But there are times when difficult choices have to be made. Recently, I was reluctant to support the Head Start programme sponsored by the Bush administration. Most of the money goes to big

cities like Miami which don't use it very well, rather than to places like Fort Myers [in my district] that use it better. Eventually a compromise was reached. The programme would be trialled in just 8 states. The administration got my vote.

Delegate or trustee?

But to what extent should a member of Congress feel bound to represent the views of constituents, even if he or she knows what they are? Is a member of Congress merely a delegate who is mandated to vote as instructed by others? Or do Senator or House members act as trustees; having consulted their constituents do they then use their own political judgement as well?

And not all constituents' views are of equal importance. According to the noted political scientist Richard Fenno, many members view their constituents as a set of concentric circles, ranging from their closest political confidants (who Fenno calls 'the intimates'), to their strongest supporters in the electorate ('the primary constituency'), other voters who will vote for them ('the re-election constituency') and, the furthest of the circles, their state or district ('the geographic constituency'). But even the membership of the second and third 'circles' is not always clear. You can read more about Fenno's theory in *The American Congress* (Houghton Mifflin, 1999).

In an interview in the mid-1990s, a senior Democrat House member talked about a vote which had just come up on the House floor on aid to Russia. 'This passed the House by a large, bipartisan majority,' he commented. 'Now the view from the folks across the country is "no more foreign aid". But after talking with people whose judgement I respect, I decided to vote in favour.'

Delegate or trustee — it's rarely a simple choice. Few members of Congress will see themselves as strictly one or the other. What one can say, however, is that whereas the UK House of Commons seems to fit more with the so-called mandate model of representation, the US Congress appears to be something of a mixture of delegate and trustee.

Conclusion

So, how representative is Congress? If one means in terms of 'resemblance', the answer seems to be 'not very'. It is too male, too white, too old, too highly educated, and too lawyerly to be truly representative in that sense. If one means in terms of 'delegate' or 'trustee' representation, then the answer would seem to be 'some members are, some of the time.' Many Americans hold something of a paradoxical attitude when it comes to Congress. While they hold the institution as a whole in rather low esteem, they tend to be quite satisfied with *their* Senators and House member. It's as though their slogan for Congress as a whole is, 'Throw the bums out'. But when it comes to *their own* members of Congress, 'They're *not* bums'. With re-election rates running at 95% and over in the House and usually somewhere between 85% and 95% in the Senate, one could be forgiven for presuming that someone must be doing something right.

Task 1.1

Table 1.1 shows that the majority of women in Congress between 1917 and 2007 have been Democrats. Research the current number of women in both the House and Senate (it may have changed from the figures published in this book) and see if you can find out the party balance of women in each house.

Guidance
The Center for American Women and Politics (CAWP) website (**www.cawp.rutgers.edu**) will be helpful. Go to 'Facts', then look under the heading 'Facts and findings'.

Task 1.2

Table 1.5 shows that while women's representation in the US Congress has increased from 6% to 16% between 1991 and 2007, their representation in state legislatures over the same period has only increased from 18% to just over 23%. What do you think might be a reason for this?

Guidance
The clue here is to look at Table 1.2. When the representation of women took a huge leap up in 1993, from where do you think these new women members were recruited?

Task 1.3

Briefly explain the meaning of the term 'surrogate representation'. Do you think that women and racial minority members of Congress should perform this type of representation? Give reasons for your answer.

Task 1.4

Briefly explain the meaning of the term 'majority-minority district'. Do you think that this strategy is a good one or not? Give reasons for your answer.

Task 1.5

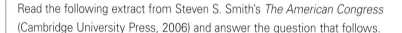

Visit the websites of other members of Congress to get further examples of constituency services provided by them.

Guidance

- Go to the House of Representatives website (**www.house.gov**). Click on the 'Representative websites' drop-down list. Click on a name, and then on 'Go'. Look for pages labelled something like 'Serving you', 'Services', or 'Constituent services'.
- Go to the Senate website (**www.senate.gov**). Click on 'Senators', then on a Senator's name in the alphabetical list. Look for pages with the same labels as for House members' websites.

Task 1.6

Read the following extract from Steven S. Smith's *The American Congress* (Cambridge University Press, 2006) and answer the question that follows.

> Many members feel a strong obligation to look out for the interests of their constituents back home, even when doing so has little effect on their re-election prospects or when there is little connection between their constituents' needs and their own policy interests. Political scientists have sometimes called the duty to behave in accordance with the wishes of constituents the delegate role. The delegate role is often contrasted with the trustee role, in which the member exercises independent judgement about questions of public policy. Of course, members seldom make a conscious philosophical judgement about whether to act as a delegate or as a trustee. For many members, behaving as a delegate comes naturally, at least on many issues. After all, most members grew up in the districts and states they serve. They often identify and empathise with their constituents, and believe that their constituents deserve good representation. But because their constituents have opinions about only a small fraction of the many policy questions Congress must confront, every member must behave like a trustee much of the time, no matter how committed he or she is to serving constituents' interests.

Using this extract, other material in the chapter, and any further information you have, write a short essay (around 250 words) in which you examine both the 'delegate' and 'trustee' models of representation and the extent to which they fit with the way members of Congress vote.

Task 1.6 (continued)

Guidance

Your essay should include:

- A clear definition and explanation of each term.
- Reasons why each model may be appropriate to understanding voting in Congress.
- Reasons why each model may *not* be appropriate to understanding voting in Congress.

Try to include one or two examples.

Further reading

- English, R. (2003) *The United States Congress*, Manchester University Press.

Why is it so hard to pass legislation through Congress?

Introduction

That it is hard to pass legislation through Congress is a fact well backed up by statistics. Of the 13,072 bills introduced during the 109th Congress (2005–06), a mere 395 (or 3%) became law. During a similar period in the UK House of Commons, 219 bills were introduced and 58 became law. (In terms of government bills only, the figure was 53 out of 69.) One just wouldn't ask the question, 'Why is it so hard to pass legislation through the UK parliament?' In Westminster, government bills are almost guaranteed passage, though private members' bills fare much less favourably.

| Table 2.1 | Number of bills introduced and laws enacted, 2001–06 |

	107th Congress 2001–02	108th Congress 2003–04	109th Congress 2005–06
Bills introduced	8,948	10,699	13,072
Laws enacted	377 (4%)	498 (5%)	395 (3%)

The reasons for the difficulties in passing legislation through the US Congress are mainly institutional and structural; that is to say, it's more to do with the way the system is designed than for reasons of gross inefficiency. It's not so much that the system doesn't work, but rather that the system is *designed* not to work. And, as we shall see, the crux of the matter is tied up with the constitutional system of checks and balances — the 'separated institutions, sharing powers' of which Richard Neustadt spoke.

The reasons why it is so hard to pass legislation in Congress can be considered using seven headings. We shall start with those that concern the legislative process itself.

(1) The process itself is complicated

'The hurdles to enacting legislation are substantial,' states Burdett Loomis in the recent edition of his scholarly work *The Contemporary Congress* (Wadsworth, 2004). 'Perhaps the most remarkable feature of the legislative process is how much it is stacked against the enactment of new law,' states congressional scholar Steven Smith (*The American Congress*, Houghton Mifflin, 1999). And how right they are. Although the legislative process in Congress is analogous to that within the UK parliament — there are three readings and a committee stage in both — the differences are so fundamental as to make the outcomes altogether different.

The most important difference in the process is the positioning and significance of the committee stage. Whereas in the UK parliament the committee stage comes *after* the second reading, and is done by essentially ad hoc (temporary), generalist committees, in the US Congress the committee stage comes *before* the second reading and is done by permanent, policy specialist committees. The congressional standing committees have virtual life-and-death power over bills as well as full power of amendment. Their members are deferred to by ordinary House and Senate members, who will often bow to the specialist knowledge of committees.

But it is a mistake to think that it is just the legislative process that makes it difficult to pass legislation through Congress. That in itself does not in any way account for why a mere 5% of bills are passed.

(2) There is a need for super-majorities at certain stages

In his book *Pivotal Politics: The Theory of US Lawmaking* (University of Chicago Press, 1998), Keith Krehbiel lays down what he calls three crucial 'pivots' in Congress:
- Any bill must find a majority in both houses.
- Any bill must find a majority of three-fifths in the Senate.
- Any bill must, if it is opposed by the president, find a majority of two-thirds in both houses.

The first point is obvious. All bills must pass votes at the end of their second and third readings — and possibly gain the approval of the conference committee report — before they can be passed to the president for his signature. In these votes, a simple majority of those voting is required.

The second point relates to the power of filibuster in the Senate. To end a filibuster, three-fifths of the entire Senate (i.e. 60 Senators) are required to vote

in favour. So, for example, when on 21 December 2005 the Senate was voting on the conference committee report of the Fiscal Year 2006 Defense Appropriations Bill, the vote was 56–44 to end the filibuster. But that was 4 votes short of the 60 votes required. Thus, although 56 Senators wanted to pass the bill, the bill was not passed.

The third point relates to the president's power of veto. To override the president's veto, both houses must vote in favour by a two-thirds majority. Thus, back in 1997 when President Clinton vetoed the Late-Term Abortion Ban Bill, the House voted to override the President's veto by 296 to 132, 11 votes over the two-thirds required. But in the Senate the vote to override was only 64 to 36 in favour, 3 votes short of the required two-thirds. So, although 360 members of Congress wanted to go ahead with the legislation, it was the 168 members who did not want the bill who won the day — with the President's support.

These examples show how legislation can be frustrated by a small minority of Congress. That makes it difficult to pass legislation. Supporters have a much higher bar to clear than do opponents.

(3) Both houses possess equal power in passing legislation

Not only is the legislative process complicated — it is made more difficult to negotiate by the fact that both houses of Congress have equal power when it comes to legislation. It is often rightly said that the Senate is more powerful — and therefore more prestigious — than the House of Representatives. This derives from the Senate's exclusive powers with regards to the confirmation of the president's appointments to both the executive and the judiciary as well as the Senate's power to ratify treaties. But when it comes to the passage of legislation, both houses have equal powers.

Therefore, whereas in the UK parliament it is essentially only one chamber that has to give its wholehearted consent to legislation, in the US Congress that consent must be forthcoming from both houses. Neither chamber has any way of out-manoeuvring or overriding the other. Bills must be approved by the standing committees of *both* chambers. Bills must be voted for by majorities at the second and third readings in *both* chambers. A conference committee report must be approved by majority votes in *both* chambers. Should the president veto the bill, a two-thirds majority to override this veto must be secured in *both* chambers.

(4) The two houses may be controlled by different parties

It is likely to be even more difficult to pass legislation through Congress when different parties control the two houses, as for example was the case between mid-2001 and the end of 2002, when a Democrat-controlled Senate faced a Republican-controlled House. The situation was reversed — a Republican-controlled Senate and a Democrat-controlled House — in the 6-year period from 1981 to 1987.

This divided Congress would not matter so much if one house enjoyed superior power in the passage of legislation. In the UK parliament immediately following the 1997 general election, there was a Labour-controlled Commons but a Conservative-controlled Lords. But in the UK system of government, the Commons is superior in power to the Lords when it comes to the passage of legislation, so a situation of divided party control matters much less than it does in the US Congress.

During a period of divided party control in Congress, the House and Senate will be working to different agendas and their committees will be chaired by followers of different political ideologies. For instance, in the 18-month period of divided party control during 2001–02, the standing committees dealing with agriculture were chaired in the House by Republican Larry Combest of Texas, but in the Senate by Democrat Tom Harkin of Iowa. This conservative Republican and liberal Democrat have little, if anything, in common except an interest in agriculture. Quite simply, it was easier to get legislation through these committees when the Senate committee was chaired by Indiana Republican Dick Lugar.

(5) The presidency and Congress may be controlled by different parties

'Divided government' is where one party controls the White House and the other party controls (usually) both houses of Congress. This was the position in American government for much of the period between 1969 (the start of Nixon's first term) and 2001 (the end of Clinton's second term). Of these 32 years, divided government was in place for 20 of them. For 6 years during this period (1981–87), the president's party controlled only one house in

Congress. For only 6 years (1977–81 and 1993–94) did one party — the Democrats — control the White House and both houses of Congress.

The difficulty here comes at the beginning and end of the legislative process. When the president delivers his State of the Union Address to a Congress controlled by the 'opposition' party, it is difficult for him to get action on his legislative agenda. One saw this with Nixon, Ford and the first George Bush, all of whom faced divided government for the whole of their terms of office. We saw it again during Bill Clinton's second term and in George W. Bush's last 2 years. The president wants one thing, but Congress wants something else. In the late 1990s, with Democrat Bill Clinton facing a Republican Congress, the President wanted an increase in the minimum wage while the Republican Congress wanted cuts in federal programmes.

| Table 2.2 | Presidential vetoes: President and Congress of same party and divided government compared, 1961–2005 |

President	Dates	Number of years	Number of vetoes
President and Congress of same party			
Kennedy	1961–63	3	12
Johnson	1963–68	5	16
Carter	1977–81	4	13
Clinton	1993–95	2	0
Bush (43)	2001–05*	4	1
TOTALS		**18**	**42**
Divided government			
Nixon	1969–74	6	26
Ford	1974–77	2	48
Reagan	1987–89	2	8
Bush (41)	1989–93	4	29
Clinton	1995–2001	6	36
TOTALS		**20**	**147**

*The Senate was controlled by the Democrats between May 2001 and December 2002.

The difficulties of divided government are accentuated again at the end of the legislative process, in the use of the presidential veto. As Table 2.2 shows, presidential vetoes are far more frequent during periods of divided government than during those periods when one party controls both president and Congress. The 18 years between 1961 and 2005 when the president and Congress were of the same party saw 42 presidential vetoes, an average of just over 2 per year. But the 20 years of divided government during the same period saw 147 presidential vetoes, an average of over 7 per year. And although 25 of those vetoes were overridden, compared with only 2 during united government, that still meant that far more bills were defeated during divided government.

(6) Party discipline in Congress is comparatively weak

Even when presidents do enjoy a majority of their own party in both houses of Congress, there is no guarantee of legislative success. It can still be hard to pass legislation.

When Bill Clinton arrived in the White House in January 1993, his Democrats enjoyed an 82-seat majority in the House and a 16-seat majority in the Senate. At the start of the congressional session that January, the President announced six legislative priorities: an economic stimulus package; a deficit reduction package; political reform, including campaign finance reform; a national service bill; welfare reform; and — top of his agenda — healthcare reform. During the next 2 years, only two of those six legislative priorities passed, and healthcare — his legislative flagship — was not one of them.

Bill Clinton being sworn in as president at his inauguration ceremony in January 1993

In his first State of the Union Address, President Clinton had even gone so far as to brandish a pen before Congress and warn:

> If you send me [healthcare] legislation that does not guarantee every American private health insurance that can never be taken away, you will force me to take this pen, veto the legislation, and we'll come right back here and start all over again.

The President needn't have worried, as Congress never got anywhere near sending him healthcare legislation. It never even got out of the committee rooms in either chamber. And it's not just a Bill Clinton problem. Ask Jimmy Carter about his energy legislation or George W. Bush about social security reform.

Most votes in Congress are of a bipartisan nature: one group of Democrats and Republicans voting against another group of Democrats and Republicans. Just as Clinton's healthcare proposals were scuppered by discontented members of his own party, so the first George Bush's 1990 tax increases were passed only with the support of the opposition party — the Democrats.

It is true to say that most big-ticket legislation is passed through Congress by quite large, bipartisan majorities — take, for example, George W. Bush's education reform (2001). We shall look at this piece of legislation as a case study at the end of this chapter.

(7) Power in Congress has become more decentralised

Back in the 1950s and 1960s, it was possible to pass legislation through Congress merely by securing the support of a few key congressional leaders — the Speaker, the Majority Leader and the relevant committee chairman, who were known as 'Kings of the Hill'. No longer. The 1970s, 1980s and 1990s were decades of decentralisation in Congress. Power moved away from a few powerful committee chairmen to subcommittee chairmen, and to ordinary members of Congress. In the words of Professor Anthony King: 'the powerful "few" became the considerably less powerful "many"'. This makes passing legislation through Congress much more difficult. John Ehrlichman, an aide to President Nixon in the early 1970s, likened putting coalitions together in Congress to support legislation as 'laborious, step by step work, like putting together tiles in a great mosaic'. And it was Anthony King, again, who likened the whole process of trying to get the president and Congress to work together on legislation as 'like trying to sew buttons on a custard pie!'

There have been some signs since 2001 that this situation may be going into reverse and Congress could once again become a more centralised, organised place and therefore potentially easier to manage. The former Republican Speaker of the House, Dennis Hastert, was prepared to use his power to get the people he wanted appointed to leadership posts in the House. This was also true during the tenure of House Majority Leader Tom DeLay. But it is way too early to tell whether or not this is a trend, or merely a passing blip.

Case study: 'No Child Left Behind' Act

There are, therefore, seven reasons why it is so hard to pass legislation through Congress. Let us look in some detail at one landmark piece of legislation that passed through the 107th Congress in 2001 — the 'No Child Left Behind' Act, which was George W. Bush's education reform bill.

Bush had made education reform a centrepiece both of his time as Texas state governor and of his 2000 presidential campaign. So it was no surprise when, as president, he made it a top and early priority in 2001. The basic purpose of the reform was to provide more money to states and more flexibility in spending it. But the states would have to account for their use of this money with improved performance, specifically by improving student test scores to be measured by state testing plans.

The most controversial aspect of the reform was the provision of school vouchers, which would allow parents to have a voucher to the value of what it would cost to educate their child in a public (i.e. state-run) school to use towards the cost of education in a private school. This was controversial for two reasons. First, the teachers' unions saw it as money lost to the public school system — and the teachers' unions are a powerful lobby within the Democratic Party. Second, 'private schools' often meant 'religious schools', and therefore Democrats saw school vouchers as being contrary to the important doctrine of 'separation of church and state'.

However, the beginnings of the legislation were undoubtedly bipartisan. President Bush worked hard to court the support of two influential Democrats, Senator Edward Kennedy of Massachusetts and Congressman George Miller of California, respectively the ranking Democrat members of the Senate and House committees that would be dealing with the legislation.

Committee stage

The legislation kicked off in the Senate on 8 March 2001, when the Senate Health, Education, Labor and Pensions Committee voted 20–0 to approve

what was officially known as the Elementary and Secondary Education Bill (numbered S1), but often referred to by Republicans as the 'No Child Left Behind' Bill, using George W. Bush's phrase from the 2000 election campaign.

Table 2.3 'No Child Left Behind' Bill timeline

Date	Action
8 March 2001	Senate Committee approves bill S1 (22–0)
22 March	House Committee begins consideration of bill HR1
3 May	Senate begins debate on bill S1
9 May	House Committee approved bill HR1 (41–7)
17 May	House Rules Committee grants HR1 an open rule
22–23 May	2-day debate on HR1 on House floor
23 May	House approves the bill HR1 (384–45)
24 May	*Senator Jeffords switches to Independent, handing control of the Senate to the Democrats*
5 June	President Bush meets with 9 leading Senators at the White House to discuss upcoming Senate debate
6–14 June	Senate continues debate on bill S1
14 June	Senate approves S1 (91–98)
19 July	First meeting of 39-member conference committee to merge S1 and HR1
1 August	President gives speech to National Urban League
2 August	President meets at White House with 'big four' conferees
11 September	*Attacks on New York and Washington DC*
11 December	Conference committee agrees final version of bill
13 December	House approves conference report (381–41)
18 December	Senate approves conference report (87–10)
8 January, 2002	President signs bill into law

Various amendments proposed in the Senate committee were rejected. These included amendments offered by:

- Democrat Senator Patty Murray of Washington, to authorise a 7-year extension of the class-size reduction programme that had been funded for the 3 years since 1998.
- Republican Senator Jeff Sessions of Alabama, to allow federal funds to be used to train school employees and parents to look for signs of weapons or indications that a student might turn violent.
- Democrat Senator Chris Dodd of Connecticut, to increase the authorisation of funds for after-school programmes from $846 million to $1.5 billion.

The Senate version of the bill did not include provision of school vouchers, preferring to leave that fight until later in the process.

Action then switched to the House, where John Boehner of Ohio, chair of the Education and the Workforce Committee, introduced the bill on 22 March. The House version of the bill (numbered HR1) was much closer to the White House position. It both included school vouchers and called for aid to faith-based organisations.

Over the next few weeks both the Senate and House tried to come up with a bipartisan compromise version of the bill. This had the result of moving the bill closer to the Democrats' position. For example, school vouchers were dropped and funding levels increased — two cornerstone Democrat positions. But this meant that some conservative interest groups, which had up till now been supporting the bill, came out against it. The Family Research Council, the Eagle Forum and the Traditional Values Coalition, for example, all now said they opposed the bill.

On 9 May, the House committee approved the bill by a vote of 41 to 7. The 7 dissenting votes were cast by 6 conservative Republicans who thought the bill had been watered down too much, and 1 Democrat. But for the White House, and for most Republicans, it was enough that the bill was on the move. Compromise is an important ingredient of moving legislation through Congress. David Nather, writing in *Congressional Quarterly* (12 May 2001), stated that 'Bush is following the same strategy he used [successfully] on tax cuts: shoot for Mars, hit the moon and declare victory.' The Democrats, for their part, pulled in enough moderate Republicans to make some significant amendments at the committee stage in the House. These included:
- major increases in funding for special education
- increased aid to poor schools
- a mentoring scheme for teachers
- the removal of school vouchers

The school vouchers clause had been removed by the House Education Committee on 2 May in a 27–20 vote. Five Republicans had joined with the committee's 22 Democrats in discarding this key provision. The ranking Democrat member George Miller described vouchers as a method to 'siphon off the limited resources of the public school system.' But Committee Chair John Boehner saw them as 'an academic life preserver for children in sinking schools'. Boehner vowed to fight again for the school voucher programme when the bill reached the floor of the House of Representatives.

But none of this seemed to bother the White House. True, it issued a statement decrying the additional spending that had been added. But it never threatened

to veto the measure were it to be passed in its current form, a tactic often used at this stage by President Clinton. 'The bill is manifestation of the President's proposals,' said Bush education adviser Sandy Kress. 'I believe 90–95% of his proposal is in this bill.' The President issued a statement on the day the House Committee approved the bill, praising its 'monumental reforms that promote real accountability, annual testing and funding flexibility'. It sounded like an endorsement, not a veto threat.

House Rules Committee

Having gained so much bipartisan support, it appeared at this stage as if the bill would sail to a quick victory. The House Rules Committee granted the bill an open rule (i.e. allowing amendments), but mainly allowed only those amendments to be debated with which it disagreed and which the House Republican leadership was pretty sure would fail on the House floor. As David Nather commented: 'The House has greater control over the process because it has a Rules Committee that can limit the number of amendments.'

House floor debate and votes

After a 2-day debate, the House passed the bill on 23 May by a vote of 384–45. The 45 'no' votes were cast by 34 conservative Republicans, 10 liberal Democrats and 1 Independent. Thus, in the California state delegation, there were 'no' votes from both conservative Republican Richard Pombo and liberal Democrat Maxine Waters. Over those 2 days, there were actually 17 votes on the bill HR1, the 17th being the one to approve its passage. Others concerned various amendments. Some were approved, and others failed, as is shown in Table 2.4.

Table 2.4	**Examples of amendments approved and rejected at second reading in the House of Representatives**

Examples of amendments approved by the House at second reading	Examples of amendments rejected by the House at second reading
• Publication of school improvement reports (361–67) • All school construction resulting from bill to use US-made steel (415–9)	• School vouchers (155–273) • Reduce funding level in bill by 11.5% (101–326)

But just as the White House was celebrating the onward march of its education reform package, an event on Capitol Hill threw everything into turmoil. On 24 May, Republican Senator James Jeffords announced that he was quitting the

Republican Party and would sit as an Independent. Up until then, the Senate had been split 50–50 along party lines, with Vice-President Dick Cheney casting his tiebreaking vote to make the Republicans the majority party. But with Jeffords no longer sitting as a Republican, the Democrats held a 50–49 advantage. Democrat Senator Edward Kennedy then became chair of the Senate Education Committee. Senate Democrats wanted to move ahead with their own legislative priorities, which did not include the President's education reforms.

Senate floor debate and votes

The Senate had begun to debate its bill (S1) at the second reading stage on 3 May. On Tuesday 5 June, President Bush summoned 9 leading Senators to the White House for a meeting with him in the cabinet room. The group included Democrats such as Ted Kennedy, Republicans like Bill Frist, and Independent James Jeffords — his first visit to the White House since his party switch cost the Republicans control of the Senate. The purpose of the meeting was for the President to lay out his current position as the Senate prepared to return to floor consideration of bill S1, on the day following the Memorial Day recess.

The Senate debated the bill on Wednesday 6 and Thursday 7 June, and continued for 3 days the following week — Tuesday, Wednesday and Thursday, from 12 to 14 June. This meant that almost 6 weeks had been devoted to debating the bill on the Senate floor. On 14 June, the Senate passed bill S1 by 91 votes to 8. The 8 'no' votes were cast by some disenchanted conservative Republicans (like Jesse Helms of North Carolina), who thought the bill was too watered down from the original proposal, and a couple of liberal Democrats (like Ernest 'Fritz' Hollings of South Carolina), who thought it didn't go far enough.

The President still sounded bullish. 'The reforms in this [Senate] bill reflect the core principles of my education agenda: accountability, flexibility, local control and more choices for parents,' he said in a statement from the White House.

Conference committee

But the two bills passed in each chamber — HR1 and S1 — had significant differences. The most startling was in terms of funding. Whereas the Senate bill provided for a $14.4 billion increase in funding in Fiscal Year 2002, the House bill provided for only $4.6 billion. But there were policy differences too. For example, the Senate bill provided $181 billion over 10 years for special education for children with disabilities. The House bill made no provision for special education at all.

The bills therefore needed to be referred to a conference committee to reconcile the differences between the House and Senate versions. The 39-member conference committee had its first meeting on 19 July under its chair, Republican Congressman John Boehner — the chair of the House Education Committee that had earlier considered the bill in the House. All the other 13 House conferees were also drawn from House Education Committee — 7 other Republicans plus 6 Democrats. By the time Congress went home for its summer recess in early August, little progress had been made. President Bush summoned four of the leading conferees — Senators Kennedy (D) and Gregg (R), along with Congressmen Boehner (R) and Miller (D) — to the White House on 2 August to discuss how to move things along when Congress reconvened in September. The day before, the President had used a speech to the National Urban League to call again for education reform which ensured that improved student performance was 'rigorous, achievable and targeted to all groups.'

It was at this point that yet another unconnected event made a significant impact on the bill's chances of passage — September 11. At a time when domestic priorities were being quickly pushed onto the backburner to make way for more pressing issues of national security, the future of the education reform bill looked somewhat bleak. David Nather, writing in *Congressional Quarterly* in late October, put it like this:

> In less chaotic times, before September 11, the education bill was viewed as a must-pass piece of legislation. Now, with most of Congress focused on anti-terrorism legislation, airline security, an economic stimulus package and measures to combat bio-terrorism, education has slipped down several notches.

'Negotiations on education overhaul expose deep split over funding level', read a *Congressional Quarterly* headline following the conference committee meeting on 25 September. But this meeting did gain agreement on three relatively minor issues: reading programmes, after-school programmes, and Charter schools.

By 1 December, the conferees were saying that 'the end is near' with only one outstanding issue to be resolved — that of funding. The following week, on 11 December, the conference committee wrapped up its work — it had taken 5 months — and sent the agreed version of the bill for votes in both chambers. 'I commend the conferees for agreeing on a series of profound reforms to help provide our children [with] the best education possible,' said the President in a statement. The final version of the bill provided for a $4.3 billion increase in funding in Fiscal Year 2002 — this was below the figures of both the original Senate and House versions, but reflected the changed domestic circumstances following 9/11. However, the bill did include many aspects of the President's original plan:

- all children in 3rd to 8th Grade to be tested in reading and maths each year
- each state to set goals for schools to raise student achievement for children across many demographic groups
- new federal sanctions for schools that fail to meet these goals
- an early-reading programme
- increased accountability on hiring quality teachers
- increased funding for teaching English to immigrant children

Final passage votes

The House adopted the conference report by 381–41 on 13 December. The 41 'no' votes were cast by 33 Republicans, 6 Democrats and 2 Independents. Of the 45 House members who voted 'no' on 23 May, 28 still voted 'no' on the conference report, 14 voted 'yes' and the remaining 3 did not vote or declare a position.

On 18 December, the Senate adopted the conference report by 87–10. The 10 'no' votes were cast by 3 Republicans, 6 Democrats and Independent James Jeffords. Only 2 of these — Republicans Bennett of Utah and Voinovich of Ohio — had also voted 'no' in June.

The President issued an immediate statement:

I commend members of Congress for acting boldly and in an overwhelmingly bipartisan way to help make sure no child in America is left behind. These historic reforms will improve our public schools by creating an environment where every child can learn through real accountability, unprecedented flexibility for states and school districts, greater local control, more options for parents, and more funding for what works.

Many share in the credit for making these reforms a reality. I look forward to standing side-by-side with the bipartisan leadership — Congressman Boehner, Senator Kennedy, Senator Gregg and Congressman Miller — early next year and signing these important reforms into law.

Putting aside partisan differences and working to find common ground, we can get things done so that all our children have the opportunity for a better and brighter future.

President signs bill into law

The bill-signing ceremony came on 8 January at Hamilton High School, Hamilton, Ohio. In attendance were the Republican and Democratic members of Congress who had worked the hardest to get the bill through Congress — Republicans John Boehner and Judd Gregg along with Democrats Edward Kennedy and George Miller — as well as Education Secretary Rod Paige.

George W. Bush at the 'No Child Left Behind' bill-signing ceremony

The President used the opportunity to thank each one individually. To see President Bush and Senator Kennedy sharing a political platform is indeed a rare sight. The two have little in common, ideologically. Bush is a conservative Republican, Kennedy a liberal Democrat. But this is what is so distinctive about US politics, and especially about getting things done in Congress. It means 'reaching across the aisle', as the phrase goes — Republicans reaching out to Democrats, and vice versa. Here is President Bush speaking of Kennedy:

> And then, of course, there's Senator Edward Kennedy. The folks at the Crawford Coffee Shop [in Bush's home town in Texas] would be somewhat shocked when I told them I actually like the fellow. He is a fabulous Senator. When he's against you, it's tough. When he's with you, it is a great experience.

In his reply, Senator Kennedy repaid the compliment: 'What a difference it has made this year with your leadership.'

The President had chosen to sign the bill at Hamilton High School because it was in the hometown of John Boehner, Republican chair of the House Education Committee, who was singled out by Bush for the most lavish praise:

John did a really good job. He shepherded the bill through the process. He made sure people showed up for the meetings. He was dogged in his determination to get this bill done. It would not have happened without his leadership.

And it probably wouldn't. That is how far even a president is dependent upon others to get legislation through Congress. It had taken 10 months — from 8 March 2001 to 8 January 2002 — of hearings, conversations, debates, amendments, votes, meetings, compromises and sheer persistence. It is hard to pass legislation through Congress.

Task 2.1

Read the extract below, from the *National Journal* (15 December 2001), and then answer the questions that follow.

Lessons in bipartisanship by Richard E. Cohen

Representative John Boehner (R – Ohio), the chairman of the Education and Workforce Committee, faced a stiff challenge in assembling a bipartisan majority for his education reform bill earlier this year. Boehner said it helped significantly that he had established a good relationship with the committee ranking member George Miller (D – California), one of the House's most outspoken liberals. 'We had several meetings where I said that I wanted the committee to be more productive and have a new tone,' Boehner said. 'We came to an understanding of what our goals would be.'

But some conservative Republicans were livid about the cooperation, and 34 Republicans voted against Boehner's bill when the House approved it 384–45 in May, even though President Bush had listed education as his top domestic priority. But this week, the House and Senate were heading toward overwhelming approval of the final compromise education bill.

Before winning his House seat, Boehner served in the Ohio state legislature, which he cites as a model of bipartisan legislating. In Congress, he has usually voted the Republican line. But he took over his committee in January 2001 pledging to work with Democrats in a chamber where such cooperation has been the exception in recent years.

(a) What reason does John Boehner (pronounced 'Bayner') give for his success in putting together 'a bipartisan majority' for the education reform bill?

(b) Why do you think that 'some conservative Republicans were livid about the cooperation' with Democrats?

(c) What do we know about Boehner's earlier political career that suggests he would be happy working with Democrats as well as with fellow Republicans?

Task 2.1 (continued)

Guidance

(a) The clue is in the first paragraph, and especially in his relationship with George Miller.

(b) The clue may be in the word 'conservative'. Think about how although fellow Republicans, conservatives might be ideologically different from John Boehner.

(c) Find out about the state Boehner comes from. Where is it geographically? Is it a state that nearly always returns politicians of one party or is it a highly competitive state? See if you can find out the state's popular vote in recent presidential elections. You can do this by going to **www.uselectionatlas.org**.

Task 2.2

On page 33, there is a quotation from Burdett Loomis, in which he states that 'the hurdles to enacting legislation are substantial (from *The Contemporary Congress*, 2004).' Explain what these hurdles are and why they are 'substantial'.

Guidance

These 'hurdles' may be examined under two headings: those relating to the legislative process itself, and those relating to other institutional arrangements. You can find out about the former in the 'No Child Left Behind Act' case study and about the latter in points 2–7 of this chapter.

Task 2.3

The president has few formal powers relating to the legislative process. He can introduce legislation and then, at the end of the process, either sign or veto the bill. What actions did President George W. Bush take to facilitate the passage of his Education Reform Bill?

Guidance

You can get clues from the timeline on page 40 and from the text. You should note the actions President Bush took during the 2000 election campaign; the White House's attitude towards compromises with Democrats; statements issued by the President as the bill was proceeding; meetings held by the President; speeches and statements made by the President.

Task 2.4

In order to get legislation passed in Congress, supporters usually have to work with members of both parties. This is called 'reaching across the aisle', a phrase mentioned on page 46.

(a) Explain why the phrase 'reaching across the aisle' is used in Congress. What is its origin?

(b) Name the two Democrat politicians with whom Republicans worked most closely to get the Education Reform Bill through Congress. See if you can discover why the support of these particular Democrats was so important.

Guidance

(a) You need to think about the layout of the House and Senate chambers. If necessary, search Google Images to find photographs of these.

(b) Their importance is linked to the leadership positions they held.

Further reading

- English, R. (2003) *The United States Congress*, Manchester University Press.
- Hamilton, L. (2004) *How Congress Works*, Indiana University Press.
- Loomis, B. and Schiller, W. (2004) *The Contemporary Congress*, Thomson Wadsworth.
- Smith, S. (1999) *The American Congress*, Houghton Mifflin.

Why are congressional committees so important?

Congressional committees are not mentioned in the US Constitution. But there are an awful lot of committees and subcommittees in Congress — 199 at the last count. They have been described as the 'work horses', the 'engine rooms', and 'the central element of the congressional infrastructure'. There are different types of congressional committees: standing committees, select committees, conference committees, party committees and joint committees. Some are permanent, while others are ad hoc. Not all congressional committees are important. Indeed, it is difficult to argue that party committees and joint committees are all that significant. They tend to be organisational and procedural rather than substantive. But standing, House Rules, select and conference committees *are* important and do fit the descriptions used in the opening sentences of this chapter. Why is this so? We shall consider these four types of committee in turn to establish the reasons for their importance.

Standing committees

We begin with the most important type of congressional committee — the standing committee. There are four reasons why congressional standing committees are so important.

(1) They are permanent, policy specialist committees

Unlike their counterparts in the UK House of Commons, congressional standing committees are permanent, policy specialist committees. Their titles suggest their specialisation — for example agriculture, armed services, judiciary. Most of these 34 standing committees — there are 18 in the House and 16 in the Senate —

have subcommittees that are even more specialist. The Senate Judiciary Committee, for example, has 7 subcommittees including one for crime and drugs, another for immigration, refugees and border security, while yet another deals with terrorism, technology and homeland security.

Members of Congress seek assignments to the standing committees that are prestigious, such as the armed services or judiciary committees of each chamber. They will also want to join those that may have a connection with the interests of their constituents. Committees on transportation will, for example, attract members from states on the Interstate 95 highway corridor, from Massachusetts in the north to Florida in the south. Committees dealing with agriculture, on the other hand, are more likely to feature members from the Midwest or the South. The House Transportation and Infrastructure Committee has 6 members from New York and 7 from Pennsylvania. On the other hand, the House Agriculture Committee has 4 members from North Carolina but only 1 from Pennsylvania. The Senate Indian Affairs Committee draws its members from such states as Hawaii, North Dakota, Wyoming, Arizona and Oregon.

These interests mean that committee members are policy specialists from day one. They also seek to remain on the same committee to pursue their speciali- sation. Committee members are viewed as policy specialists by other members of Congress, who will often solicit their views before a vote takes place on the floor of either chamber.

Committee members' policy specialisations may continue later into their careers. In the early 1990s the California Congressman Norman Mineta rose to be chair of the House Transportation Committee. Ten years later he was Secretary of Transportation in the George W. Bush administration. During his one term in the Senate (1993–99), Dirk Kempthorne of Idaho served on the Environment and Public Works Committee. In 2006, he was recruited by President Bush to be Secretary of the Interior.

(2) They play a strategic role in the legislative process

In the legislative process in Congress, the committee stage — conducted by the relevant standing committee — comes *before* the second reading; that is, *before* the first main debate in the chamber. Because the first reading in each chamber is only a formality, this means that the standing committee gets to shape the bill at the start of the legislative process. By contrast, in the UK parliament, bills go to committee *after* the second reading, in other words after the full chamber has agreed on the principles of the bill.

Add to this the fact that standing committees have the full power of amendment, and the power to kill a bill by pigeonholing it, and one begins to realise why these committees are so powerful in the legislative process. The fate of pigeonholing happens to literally thousands of bills each congressional session. George W. Bush's 2003 tax cut proposals were drastically amended by committees in both houses of Congress. Bills may also be severely delayed in their passage through Congress by lengthy hearings — the fate that befell Bill Clinton's healthcare reform proposals in 1993–94.

True, the power of committees to stall legislation is not total. They are subject to the check of what is known as the discharge rule. But this rule is difficult to utilise successfully, especially in the House, where a discharge petition must be signed by an absolute majority of the House membership (218) to be successful. The procedure was used successfully in January 2002, in relation to the campaign finance reform bill then making slow — but eventually successful — progress through the House. Mostly the wishes of the standing committees win the day. Forty years ago, in the mid-1960s, an eminent commentator described congressional standing committees as 'the Lords Proprietors of the Congress'. The term was — and still is — only a slight exaggeration.

(3) They play a vital role in the scrutiny function of Congress

As we have seen, not only do standing committees play an important role in the legislative and representative functions of Congress, they also have a key role in the third function of Congress — that of the scrutiny of the executive branch of government. In the UK parliament, this function is shared between the committees and the chambers. Indeed, the more public performance of this function takes place on the floor of the House of Commons at Question Time. But in a system of government like that in the USA, which is based on the *separation* rather than the *fusion* of powers, it is really only in the committee rooms that this function can be truly pursued. There can be no Question Time in either chamber of Congress, quite simply because there is no one there to question. It is only in the committee rooms — and essentially the standing committee rooms — where members of the executive branch can be regularly called to account.

Table 3.1 shows that during 2005, members of President Bush's cabinet made 67 appearances in front of congressional standing committees. Secretary of the Treasury John Snow made 4 appearances in 3 days in early February, appearing before the Senate Finance and House Ways and Means committees on the 8th, the House Budget Committee on the 9th, and the Senate Budget Committee on the 10th. The Senate Appropriations Committee heard from 5 different cabinet officers during a 3-day period in March — the secretaries of the Interior, Transportation, Labor, Veterans Affairs, and Health and Human Services.

Table 3.1 **Appearances by Bush cabinet members at congressional standing committees, 2005**

Date	Committee	Cabinet officer
3 February	Senate Agriculture	Secretary of Agriculture
8 February	Senate Finance	Secretary of the Treasury
	House Ways and Means	Secretary of the Treasury
9 February	House Budget	Secretary of the Treasury
10 February	Senate Budget	Secretary of the Treasury
15 February	Senate Armed Services	Secretary of Energy
16 February	House Armed Services	Secretary of Defense
	Senate Foreign Relations	Secretary of State
	Senate Finance	Secretary of Health and Human Services
	Senate Appropriations	Secretary of Defense
17 February	House International Relations	Secretary of State
	Senate Appropriations	Secretary of State
	Senate Armed Services	Secretary of Defense
	House Ways and Means	Secretary of Health and Human Services
2 March	Senate Appropriations	Secretary of Education
	House Financial Services	Secretary of Housing and Urban Development
3 March	Senate Energy and Natural Resources	Secretary of Energy
9 March	Senate Homeland Security	Secretary of Homeland Security
10 March	House Armed Services	Secretary of Defense
	Senate Appropriations	Secretary of the Interior
15 March	Senate Appropriations	Secretary of Transportation
	Senate Appropriations	Secretary of Labor
	Senate Appropriations	Secretary of Veterans Affairs
16 March	Senate Appropriations	Secretary of Health and Human Services
	House Ways and Means	Secretary of Labor
5 April	Senate Judiciary	Attorney General
6 April	House Financial Services	Secretary of Commerce
	House Financial Services	Secretary of Housing and Urban Development

Date	Committee	Cabinet officer
7 April	Senate Banking, Housing and Urban Affairs	Secretary of Housing and Urban Development
	Senate Banking, Housing	Secretary of the Treasury
13 April	House Homeland Security	Security of Homeland Security
	House Financial Services	Secretary of the Treasury
	House Financial Services	Secretary of Housing and Urban Development
14 April	Senate Health, Education, Labor	Secretary of Education
	Senate Health, Education, Labor	Secretary of Labor
	Senate Appropriations	Secretary of Housing and Urban Development
19 April	House Financial Services	Secretary of the Treasury
20 April	Senate Appropriations	Security of Homeland Security
21 April	Senate Banking, Housing and Urban Affairs	Secretary of Housing and Urban Development
26 April	Senate Appropriations	Secretary of the Treasury
27 April	Senate Appropriations	Secretary of Defense
11 May	House Financial Services	Secretary of Housing and Urban Development
12 May	Senate Appropriations	Secretary of State
26 May	Senate Banking, Housing and Urban Affairs	Secretary of the Treasury
9 June	House Government Reform	Secretary of Homeland Security
16 June	Senate Banking, Housing and Urban Affairs	Secretary of Housing and Urban Development
23 June	Senate Finance	Secretary of the Treasury
	House Armed Services	Secretary of Defense
	Senate Armed Services	Secretary of Defense
13 July	House Financial Services	Secretary of the Treasury
14 July	Senate Homeland Security	Secretary of Homeland Security
	Senate Banking, Housing and Urban Affairs	Secretary of the Treasury
19 July	Senate Commerce	Secretary of Homeland Security
20 July	Senate Budget	Secretary of Health and Human Services
31 July	Senate Banking, Housing and Urban Affairs	Secretary of the Treasury
21 September	Senate Agriculture	Secretary of Agriculture
29 September	House Armed Services	Secretary of Defense
	Senate Armed Services	Secretary of Defense
	House Education and Workforce	Secretary of Education
16 October	Senate Banking, Housing and Urban Affairs	Secretary of the Treasury

Date	Committee	Cabinet officer
18 October	Senate Judiciary	Secretary of Homeland Security
	Senate Judiciary	Secretary of Labor
19 October	Senate Foreign Relations	Secretary of State
26 October	Senate Budget	Secretary of Health and Human Services
30 October	Senate Banking, Housing and Urban Affairs	Secretary of the Treasury
2 November	Senate Appropriations	Secretary of Health and Human Services
4 November	House Government Reform	Secretary of Health and Human Services

These investigative hearings before congressional standing committees often touch on the most important issues of the day. For example, in February 2006 Attorney General Alberto Gonzales appeared before the Senate Judiciary Committee to defend the controversial National Security Agency's (NSA) eavesdropping programme as part of the 'War on Terror'. The respected Washington journal *CQ Weekly* headlined the hearing: 'Congress lets White House know it won't rubber-stamp claims of executive branch authority in NSA spying case.' The committee was especially vexed about the administration's failure to consult with Congress about the intelligence-gathering activities. The ranking Democrat on the committee told Gonzales:

Under our Constitution, Congress is a co-equal branch of government, and we make the laws. If you believe you need new laws, then come and tell us. If Congress agrees, we'll amend the law. If you do not even attempt to persuade Congress to amend the law then you're required to follow the law as it's written.

Even Republicans pitched in with criticism of the way the Bush administration had failed to ask Congress for new or amended legislation rather than just operating in secrecy. This was Mike DeWine of Ohio:

From a constitutional as well as from a policy point of view, the President and the American people would be stronger — this country would be stronger and the President would be stronger — if he did so, if he had come to Congress for such specific statutory authorisation.

But the Attorney General was equally feisty:

Our enemy is listening. And I cannot help but wonder if they aren't shaking their heads in amazement at the thought that anyone would imperil such a sensitive programme by leaking its existence in the first place — and smiling at the prospect that we might now disclose even more or perhaps unilaterally disarm ourselves of a key tool in the war on terror.

In a space of 3 days, the Attorney General appeared before both the Senate and House Judiciary Committees as well as at a closed-door session of the Senate Intelligence Committee.

(4) They begin the process of confirming appointments in the Senate

The Constitution gives the Senate the exclusive power to 'advise and consent' to numerous appointments made by the president. It must confirm many top-level executive branch appointments, as well as all appointments to the federal judiciary. And it is in the relevant Senate standing committee that the confirmation process begins. So, for example, when Alberto Gonzales was appointed as Attorney General by President Bush in January 2005, his confirmation process began at the Senate Judiciary Committee, which eventually split 10–8 along party lines to recommend the nomination to the full chamber.

Because standing committee members are regarded by their Senate colleagues as policy experts, the full chamber vote often reflects the vote in the committee. In the Gonzales nomination, therefore, the floor vote was 60–36, with 54 Republicans joined by 6 moderate Democrats voting in favour of his confirmation. Should a standing committee vote to not recommend confirmation, then the outlook for the nomination on the Senate floor is bleak. In 1989, the Senate Armed Services Committee voted 9–11 against recommending the confirmation of John Tower as Secretary of Defense. The Senate chamber then rejected the nomination by 47 votes to 53.

The standing committee kept the busiest in this function is the Senate Judiciary Committee. It not only holds hearings on the many Justice Department appointees, but also deals with all the appointments to the federal judiciary. The media tend to focus only on appointments to the Supreme Court, and vacancies there occur on average only once every 2 years. By coincidence, there were no vacancies in the Supreme Court between 1994 and 2005. So you might have thought that the confirmation of federal judges was not a particularly arduous function. Far from it. The president nominates some 50–60 federal judges per year. The first President Bush, for example, nominated 210 federal judges in his 4-year term (1989–93) — 2 to the Supreme Court, 60 to the Courts of Appeal, and 148 to the District Courts. Lower federal court nominations can prove controversial, as when the Senate rejected Bill Clinton's nomination of Ronnie White to the US District Court in 1999.

But it is when a vacancy appears on the Supreme Court that the role of the Senate Judiciary Committee is shown to the full. After an 11-year moratorium, 2 vacancies occurred in late-2005, with first the retirement of Associate Justice Sandra Day O'Connor and then the death of Chief Justice William Rehnquist. So between September 2005 and January 2006 the Senate Judiciary Committee had to conduct two confirmation hearings, one on John Roberts and the other on Samuel Alito. Again, the conclusions of the committee proved to be similar to the conclusions of the Senate as a whole. On the nomination of John Roberts, the Senate Judiciary Committee voted by 13 votes to 5 to recommend his confirmation. The full Senate confirmed him by a vote of 78–22. On the nomination of Samuel Alito, the committee voted by 10–8 to recommend his confirmation. The full Senate confirmed him by a vote of 58–42. These examples, too, show the importance of the standing committees in shaping decisions on the floor of the chamber.

House Rules Committee

Although it is one of the standing committees of the House of Representatives, the House Rules Committee is so different from other House standing committees that it deserves to be discussed separately. The House Rules Committee is a timetabling committee, deciding the order of business on the House floor. It is far smaller than other House committees and does not have the same party balance. Currently its mere 13 members are made up of 9 Democrats and 4 Republicans.

Table 3.2 **Closed rules, 1981–2002**

Congress	Dates	Party controlling White House	Party controlling Congress	% of rules that were 'closed'
97th	1981–82	Republican	Divided*	25
98th	1983–84	Republican	Divided*	32
99th	1985–86	Republican	Divided*	43
100th	1987–88	Republican	Democrat	46
101st	1989–90	Republican	Democrat	55
102nd	1991–92	Republican	Democrat	66
103rd	1993–94	**Democrat**	**Democrat**	**70**
104th	1995–96	Democrat	Republican	42
105th	1997–98	Democrat	Republican	47
106th	1999–2000	Democrat	Republican	49
107th	2001–02	**Republican**	**Republican**/divided**	**63**

*Between 1981 and 1987, Democrats controlled the House, and Republicans controlled the Senate.
**Between June 2001 and December 2002, Republicans controlled the House, and Democrats controlled the Senate.

Source: Burdett Loomis and Wendy Schiller, *The Contemporary Congress*, Thomson and Wadworth, 2004, page 132

A committee dealing with floor timetables and procedure sounds spectacularly uninteresting. But it has enormous influence on the whole legislative process. Congressman John Dingell, a Democrat from Michigan, once remarked: 'If you let me write procedure and I let you write substance, I'll win every time.'

Most significantly, it is the House Rules Committee that sets time limits for floor debate and decides whether or not amendments can be offered, and, if so, which ones. If a bill is given a 'closed rule', no amendments are allowed. An 'open rule' allows amendments. The House leadership sees 'closed rules' as a way of keeping tight control on its legislative agenda. As Table 3.2 shows, when there is divided government in Washington — the White House and Congress are controlled by different parties — 'open rules' are more frequent, as the president's party tries to make bipartisan deals. But when one party controls both branches of government, the majority party is often tempted to steamroll its legislation through with 'closed rules'.

The importance of the House Rules Committee lies in its role as gatekeeper of the legislative process in the House of Representatives. Whereas other House standing committees deal only with bills in their own policy area, the House Rules Committee's power ranges far and wide to include all major legislation.

Select committees

There are a few permanent select committees in both chambers but most select committees are ad hoc. They are set up only when a matter requiring congressional investigation either cuts across the policy areas of more than one standing committee, or the investigation is likely to take so long that a standing committee does not have the time to devote to it as well as fulfil all its other functions.

On 15 September 2005 the House of Representatives approved the creation of the Select Committee to Investigate the Preparation for and Response to Hurricane Katrina, which had struck the states of Louisiana, Mississippi and Alabama earlier that month. The committee's assignment was to investigate the preparation for and response to the hurricane by federal, state and local authorities. The House Speaker named Tom Davis, a Republican from Virginia, as the committee's chair. Over the next 3 months the committee held 9 days of hearings, with witnesses including Secretary of Homeland Security Michael Chertoff and the former head of the Federal Emergency Management Agency (FEMA) Michael Brown. The committee issued its report exactly 5 months after its creation — 15 February 2006. The report stated:

The Select Committee identified failures at all levels of government that significantly undermined and detracted from the heroic efforts of first responders, private individuals and organisations, faith-based groups and others. In essence, we found that while a national emergency management system that relies on state and local governments to identify needs and request resources is adequate for most disasters, a catastrophic disaster like Katrina can and did overwhelm most aspects of the system for an initial period of time.

The catastrophic aftermath of Hurricane Katrina — national guard troops patrolling downtown New Orleans

Some select committees — those, for example on Watergate in the 1970s, the Iran-Contra affair in the 1980s and the Whitewater controversy in the 1990s — have the ability to make headlines, and even on occasion to change the course of political history. But with most investigations conducted by standing rather than select committees, the latter tend to be regarded as less important than their permanent counterparts.

Conference committees

A fourth type of congressional committee which can also be regarded as important are the ad hoc conference committees that may appear towards the end of the legislative process. With two equal legislative chambers considering bills concurrently, it is possible to end up with two different versions of the same bill — a House version and a Senate version. If these differences cannot be quickly and informally reconciled, then a conference committee will be set up to create an agreed form of the bill — agreed, that is, between the House and the Senate.

Conference committees include members of both chambers. Their membership is often drawn from the relevant standing committees that considered the bill earlier in the legislative process — another reason why standing committee members are potentially important. Because these conference committees come right at the end of the process — just before the bill is sent to the president for his signature — conference committees often craft what will be the final version of a bill. Whereas the work of standing committees can be — and often is — amended by the subsequent second and third readings in the House and Senate chambers, the conference committee's work is not amended before the bill is passed to the president for him to sign it into law. This gives the conference committee real potential importance.

To get the two versions of the same bill into identical form, lawmakers may indulge in informal legislative ping-pong, in which staff members dash from one side of the Capitol to the other, conveying suggested compromises until agreement is reached. This is what usually happens towards the end of a congressional session, as there is simply not enough time to set up a conference committee at this stage. Conference committees are used for more complex legislation that is coming through Congress in the middle of a congressional session.

But there is no set pattern of procedure for a conference committee. Chuck Brain, who served as President Clinton's legislative affairs director in the 1990s, describes the whole conference committee operation as a 'no man's land', adding, 'I've never been aware of rules for conference committees.' Some last for just a few hours, while others continue for months. The number of conferees appointed from each chamber varies widely from bill to bill. Conference committees on the federal budget can number over 200 members, while George W. Bush's 2001 tax cut legislation was dealt with by a conference committee of just 6 — 3 Senators and 3 House members. But there are no rules requiring equal numbers from the House and the Senate. It's a bit of a free-for-all.

A *National Journal* article by Richard Cohen (28 July 2001) described conference committees as being like 'a third house [of the legislature]'. A well-respected congressional scholar, he wrote:

> Imagine a shadowy arm of Congress composed of a handful of senior members who hold secret, late-night meetings to mull over key questions of federal policy. No rules govern their activities, and once they've made their decisions, their legislative handiwork is presented to rank-and-file lawmakers on a take-it-or-leave-it basis. Those sorts of practices were abolished years ago, right? Wrong. In truth, that's the way conference committees typically reconcile competing versions of House and Senate bills before Congress sends final legislation to the White House.

The way conference committees operate often does not quite equate with conventional wisdom. What frequently happens these days, according to Richard Cohen, is that 'top House and Senate Republican leaders — and perhaps a few of the relevant committee chairmen — would huddle privately to write the final version of the bills outside of the conventional conference committees, and conferees would then rubber-stamp the deals in the perfunctory meetings that were really just for show.'

Once a majority of the conference committee votes for the conference report, this is sent to each chamber for a straight up-and-down vote on the entire package — there are no amendments. Rarely does either chamber defeat a conference report. Should both chambers reject it, then the whole thing goes back to the conference committee. But once either chamber agrees to the bill, the conference committee is disbanded. So, rejection by just one chamber would mean that the bill would have to return to the start of the whole legislative process! In practice, the bill would be dead, at least for that session of Congress.

Conference committees are potentially even more difficult to negotiate when there is divided control of Congress — as, for example, there was between June 2001 and the end of 2002, with a Republican-controlled House and a Democrat-controlled Senate. Under these circumstances, reaching a compromise that will be acceptable to both chambers is all the more difficult.

Conference committees are important because they come so near the end of the whole legislative process; the House and Senate get to vote only on the whole conference package; and most major legislation is the product of a conference committee — for example George W. Bush's education reform of 2001. Conference committees really do *make* legislation.

Conclusion

We have seen that these four types of congressional committee play an important role in Congress, and that their importance touches on all three of the most

important functions of Congress — legislation, scrutiny of the executive and representation. A bill cannot be passed or a nomination confirmed without the compliance of at least one committee, and usually more. Professor Vile once commented that 'it is difficult to exaggerate the importance of these committees' in Congress.

It is difficult, maybe, but certainly possible, because committees, as powerful and important as they are, make few final decisions. In the end it is votes on the floor that pass legislation and confirm appointments. Standing committees *begin* the legislative process; Senate standing committees *begin* the confirmation process of appointments, and certainly when it comes to the questioning of executive branch members, standing committees are the only show in town. Hence, it may be possible to argue that it is in their function of executive branch scrutiny that congressional committees have their greatest importance.

Task 3.1

Using the internet, discover some examples of recent congressional committee activity, especially relating to committee hearings.

Guidance

Go to **www.house.gov**, and use the 'Committees' drop-down menu to choose a committee. Here are three possible examples:

- Agriculture: click on 'hearings and testimony' on the left.
- Foreign Affairs: look at 'committee news'.
- Judiciary: click on 'committees', 'full committee', 'legislation and oversight', then 'oversight and hearings'.

Go to **www.senate.gov**, click on 'Committees', and then choose a committee. Here are three possible examples:

- Foreign Relations: click on 'hearings'.
- Homeland Security and Governmental Affairs: click on 'hearings', then 'all hearings'.
- Judiciary: go to 'hearings'.

Task 3.2

Using the text, explain the four reasons why congressional standing committees are so important.

Guidance

The answer to this question is in the four subsections on standing committees.

Task 3.3

Study Table 3.1, which shows appearances by Bush cabinet members at congressional standing committees in 2005. List the cabinet members in order of the number of appearances they made during the year. Why do you think that the Secretaries of the Treasury and Defense, for example, made more appearances than the Secretaries of the Interior and Veterans' Affairs?

Guidance

There are 15 executive departments, the head of each being a cabinet member. All 15 cabinet members made at least one appearance, but the number of appearances varies greatly — between 1 and 15. In accounting for this, consider the relative importance of the policy areas involved.

Task 3.4

Look at the Senate Judiciary Committee's website by going to **www.senate.gov** and going to 'committees' and then 'judiciary'. Click on 'nominations'. This will show you the status of the judicial nominations of the incumbent president. By clicking on 'list of nominations and confirmation dates', you can find some examples of Senate votes on District (trial) and Circuit (appeal) Court judges. You should find instances of those judges who were easily confirmed and those whose confirmation appears to have been controversial.

Guidance

'Voice Vote' means that the judge was confirmed without the need for a recorded vote. This would indicate that all Senators supported the nomination. A judge who is confirmed but with a considerable number — more than 25 — of 'no' votes would be someone whose nomination engendered a considerable degree of controversy. Type their name into an internet search engine to see if you can find out more about them and why their nomination was controversial.

Task 3.5

The article that follows, written by Richard Cohen, contains extracts on conference committees that appeared in the *National Journal* in 2001. Read the extracts and then answer the questions.

Task 3.5 (continued)

Richard Cohen on conference committees

Imagine a shadowy arm of Congress composed of senior members who hold secret, late-night meetings to mull over key questions of federal policy. No rules govern their activities, and once they've made their decisions, their legislative handiwork is presented to rank-and-file lawmakers on a take-it-or-leave-it basis. Those sorts of practices were abolished years ago, right? Wrong. In truth it's the way conference committees typically reconcile competing versions of House and Senate bills before Congress sends final legislation to the White House.

The legislative process requires that for any bill to go the president, it must pass the House and Senate in identical form. In some cases, the two chambers will accomplish this by engaging in a form of ping-pong in which official messengers relay legislation back and forth across the Capitol, with lawmakers making changes on the floor until agreement is reached. This method is frequently used in the closing days of a Congress to save time.

Conference committees are typically reserved for more complex legislation in which bargainers from the two chambers choose to deal with each other more directly. Conference committees have no set pattern: some last a few hours, others continue for many months. The number of conferees appointed from the House and Senate may vary widely from bill to bill, and nothing requires equal numbers from each chamber. Conference committees on budget reconciliation bills can become especially cumbersome with more than 200 House and Senate members grouped into over 50 sub-conferences. At the other extreme, only three Senators and three House members served as conferees on the 2001 tax-cut package. One of them, House Ways and Means Committee ranking member Charles Rangel (D-NY) was not actually invited to participate in the working-out of the deal. The other conferees met behind closed doors over 2 gruelling days and nights at the Capitol hideaway of Senator Max Baucus (D-Montana) while the rest of Congress waited to go on its Memorial Day recess.

In his recently published book, *The Conscience of a Liberal*, Senator Paul Wellstone (D-Minnesota) explained his objections to these legislative devices: 'Conference committees, which have enormous power, are the least account-able to the public, and afford interest groups many opportunities to influence legislation.'

Task 3.5 (continued)

(a) What criticisms does Cohen offer of conference committees in the opening paragraph?

(b) Why are conference committees usually avoided in the closing days of a Congress? What procedure is used instead?

(c) In what ways do conference committees vary?

(d) What objections to conference committees did Paul Wellstone draw attention to?

Guidance

(a) Cohen mentions three criticisms, regarding accountability, timing and power.

(b) Think about the time it takes to establish a conference committee and the number of bills being passed in the closing days of a Congress.

(c) You will find this in the third paragraph.

(d) Wellstone mentions three objections to conference committees. You will find these in paragraph 4.

Further reading

- English, R. (2003) *The United States Congress*, Manchester University Press.
- Loomis, B. and Schiller, W. (2004) *The Contemporary Congress*, Thomson Wadsworth.
- Smith, S. (1999) *The American Congress*, Houghton Mifflin.

Why has Congress become more partisan?

I happened to be in Washington DC back in January 1981 on the day Ronald Reagan was sworn into office at the start of his first term as president. The days leading up to inauguration were perishingly cold, with daytime highs of around −17°C. But the northerly wind changed to a southwesterly, blowing up warm air from the Gulf of Mexico, and suddenly we were basking in spring-like temperatures of +17°C.

Reagan's inauguration also seemed to feature something of a political thaw. Here was a Republican president coming into office, while the House of Representatives had a Democrat majority. Yet here was the Speaker of the House of Representatives, Tip O'Neill — a Democrat — saying some nice things about Reagan's inaugural address and his policy agenda. The same kind of support could be heard coming from leading Senate Democrats, such as the former Senate Majority Leader Robert Byrd of West Virginia. I was shocked. I couldn't imagine British Labour Party leaders of the time saying anything encouraging or complimentary about the policy agenda of the then Conservative prime minister, Margaret Thatcher. 'Maggie, Maggie, Maggie — out! out! out!' was about as far as dialogue went in British politics at the time.

But I quickly learnt that American politics was quite different. In the USA, the ideology of the two main parties resembled a golfing umbrella — wide and many people can get under it — stark contrast to the ideology of the two main UK parties, which resembled something more like an up-turned ice cream cone. While Republicans tended to be conservative, not all conservatives tended to be Republicans. Lots of them were Democrats. Similarly, there were not only conservative Democrats like Governor George Wallace of Alabama; there were also liberal Democrats like Senator Ted Kennedy of Massachusetts. The US Congress therefore operated in an atmosphere of bipartisan cooperation.

Reagan was able to win support for his agenda from what was then referred to as 'the conservative coalition' — most Republicans, plus conservative, southern Democrats.

But that was all a long time ago. Much has changed since then — for which, as we shall see, President Reagan may have been partly responsible. These changes in party ideology and party support have significantly altered the way Congress works. The last two and a half decades have seen a move away from bipartisan politics to partisan politics in Congress. The evidence is unmistakable, and there are a number of factors that have contributed to these changes. Congress is a more partisan institution today than it was back at the start of the Reagan presidency in 1981.

Evidence that Congress has become more partisan

Before we analyse the reasons for this change, we must first substantiate the claim that Congress has become more partisan. The evidence is mainly to be found in the way members of Congress vote in both the Senate and the House of Representatives.

(1) An increase in party unity

The first piece of evidence comes in the party unity scores. This is an annual measure of the degree of party unity by each party. The figures in Table 4.1 show the percentage of roll call votes in House and Senate in which a majority of Republicans voted against a majority of Democrats. An example of such a vote would be the House vote on 28 July 2005, to pass the Central American Free Trade Agreement. Republicans voted 202–27 in favour while Democrats voted 15–187 against.

The figures in Table 4.2 show the average party unity scores for the House Republicans, House Democrats, Senate Republicans and Senate Democrats for each year between 1981 and 2006. For example, the 90% figure for House Republicans in 2005 means that in the 49% of House votes that year in which a majority of Republicans voted against a majority of Democrats (see Table 4.1), on average 90% of Republicans voted together. So the higher these percentage figures, the more party unity there is.

Table 4.1 **Frequency of party unity votes, 1981–2006**

Year	House (%)	Senate (%)
1981	37.4	47.8
1982	36.4	43.4
1983	55.6	43.7
1984	47.1	40.0
1985	61.0	49.6
1986	56.5	52.3
1987	63.7	40.7
1988	47.0	42.5
1989	56.3	35.3
1990	49.1	54.3
1991	55.1	49.3
1992	64.5	53.0
1993	65.5	67.1
1994	61.8	51.7
1995	**73.2**	**68.8**
1996	56.4	62.4
1997	50.4	50.3
1998	55.5	55.7
1999	47.3	62.8
2000	43.2	48.7
2001	40.2	55.3
2002	43.3	45.5
2003	51.7	66.7
2004	47.0	52.3
2005	49.0	62.6
2006	54.5	57.3

Highest figures in bold.

Source: *CQ Weekly*, 1 January 2007, page 39

Table 4.2 also shows that significant changes occurred both in 1993 and again in 1995. These are respectively the years when Bill Clinton became president and when the Republicans won control of Congress for the first time in 40 years. We shall see later that these two events are highly significant in the move towards increased partisanship in Congress.

| Table 4.2 | Party unity scores in the House and Senate, 1981–2006 |

	House of Representatives		Senate	
Year	Republicans (%)	Democrats (%)	Republicans (%)	Democrats (%)
1981	74	69	81	71
1982	69	72	76	72
1983	74	76	74	71
1984	71	74	78	68
1985	75	80	76	75
1986	70	79	76	72
1987	74	81	75	81
1988	74	80	68	78
1989	72	81	78	78
1990	74	81	75	80
1991	77	81	81	80
1992	79	79	79	77
1993	84	85	84	85
1994	84	83	79	84
1995	**91**	80	89	81
1996	87	80	89	84
1997	88	82	87	85
1998	86	82	86	87
1999	86	83	88	**89**
2000	88	82	89	88
2001	**91**	83	88	**89**
2002	90	86	84	83
2003	**91**	87	**94**	85
2004	88	87	90	86
2005	90	**88**	88	88
2006	88	86	86	86

Highest figures in bold.

Source: *CQ Weekly*, 1 January 2007, page 39

All four columns in Table 4.2 show their highest scores since 2001. House Republicans had a 91% party unity score in 2003; House Democrats had an 88% score in 2005; Senate Republicans had a 94% party unity score in 2003 and Senate Democrats had an 89% score in 2001.

What this means is that it is now far more likely that House Republicans will line up together than it was 25 years ago. The same goes for Senate Republicans and Senate Democrats. This suggests an increase in partisanship in both houses of Congress.

(2) An increase in the frequency of unanimous votes

Another indicator of partisanship in Congress is the dramatic rise in unanimous votes. By a unanimous vote we mean that, for example, all House Republicans vote the same way in a roll call vote. Back in the 1960s and 1970s such votes were almost unheard of. Indeed, in 1974 — the year in which President Nixon resigned — there was only one unanimous vote during the whole year in both chambers. It was scored by the Senate Democrats.

Once again, the figures show a significant rise occurring first in 1993 and again in 1995. By 2003, there were 365 unanimous votes in both chambers — 239 by the Republicans and 126 by the Democrats: an all-time record. The figures for each party caucus for 2005 are shown in Table 4.3. An instance of a unanimous vote is when all 55 Senate Republicans voted (on 29 September) in favour of the nomination of John Roberts as Chief Justice of the United States.

Table 4.3 **Unanimous votes in Congress, 2005**

	Unanimous votes by Republicans	Unanimous votes by Democrats	Total
House of Representatives	91	82	173
Senate	59	69	128
Total	**150**	**151**	**301**

(3) A decline in the number of 'conservative Democrats' and 'moderate Republicans' in both chambers

In previous decades, there was a huge overlap in the ideological spectrums of Republicans and Democrats in both houses. There were a large number of 'conservative Democrats' — like Senators John Breaux of Louisiana and Zell Miller of Georgia — who were as, if not more, conservative than many Republicans. They came almost exclusively from the South. There were also 'moderate Republicans' — often referred to as 'Rockefeller Republicans', after Governor Nelson Rockefeller of New York — who were more liberal than many Democrats. They came predominantly from the northeast. There was therefore a considerable ideological overlap between the two major parties, and a distinct lack of partisanship. This is illustrated in Figure 4.1.

Figure 4.1 **Party ideology spectrum in the 1980s**

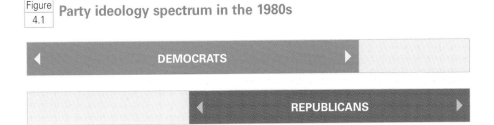

More recently, though, the Democrats have become a far more homogenously liberal party. Senators Breaux and Miller — and others like them — have retired. Their seats were usually won by Republicans who held the same conservative ideology as their Democrat predecessors. Moderate Republicans have gone the same way. In 2001, a noted Republican moderate, Senator James Jeffords of Vermont, left the Republican Party to sit as an Independent. For the next 5 years, he continued to vote consistently with the Democrats. The 2006 mid-term elections saw the retirement of Congressman Sherwood Boehlert of New York, another noted Republican moderate. As a consequence, the Republicans have become a more homogenously conservative party. There is far less ideological overlap now between the two parties (see Figure 4.2). This results in an increase in partisanship.

Figure 4.2 **Party ideology spectrum in the 2000s**

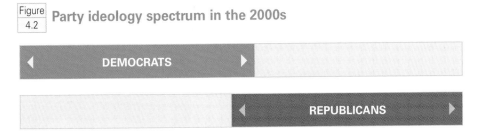

In the *National Journal* annual vote ratings for 2006, this lack of overlap between the two parties in both the House and the Senate was clearly evident. In the House, there was only 1 Democrat (Dan Boren of Oklahoma) with a 'conservative' voting record, and 9 Republicans with a 'liberal' voting record. Similarly, in the Senate, there was only 1 Democrat (Ben Nelson of Nebraska) with a 'conservative' voting record, and only 5 Republicans with a 'liberal' voting record — Lincoln Chafee of Rhode Island, Olympia Snowe and Susan Collins of Maine, Mike DeWine of Ohio and Arlen Specter of Pennsylvania.

Reasons for an increase in partisanship in Congress

Having established that there has been an increase in partisanship in Congress, and that it seems to have increased significantly in 1993, 1995 and again in 2001, we can now proceed to suggest some reasons for this phenomenon. There are three that need consideration.

(1) The break-up of 'the solid South'

We have already hinted at this. The last 45 years have seen a profound change in the politics of the South (Texas, Arkansas, Louisiana, Mississippi, Alabama, Georgia, Tennessee, Virginia, North Carolina, South Carolina and Florida). Back in 1960, when Democrat John F. Kennedy was elected president, all 11 governors of the Deep South states were Democrats, as were all 22 of the Senators, and 99 of the 106 House members. In the popular vote, Kennedy won 8 of the 11 southern states. By 1992, the Democrats still controlled a majority of these elected posts in the South, but they were not nearly so dominant: they had 8/11 governors; 13/22 Senators; and 77/125 House members. That year, a Democrat ticket made up of two southerners — Bill Clinton of Arkansas and Al Gore of Tennessee — could win only 4 of the 11 southern states.

But following the 1994 mid-term elections, the Democrats became the minority party of the South, and by 2004 the Republicans had significantly increased their dominance, as is shown in Table 4.4. In just 12 years, in the South the Democrats had lost 28 House seats, 9 Senate seats and 4 governorships. In the 4 presidential elections held during these 12 years — 1992, 1996, 2000 and 2004 — the Democrats won only 8 states in the South to the Republicans' 36. In both the 2000 and 2004 elections, the Democrats failed to win a single state in the South, and this despite the Democratic Party ticket being headed by a southerner (Al Gore) in 2000 and having a southern running-mate (John Edwards of North Carolina) in 2004.

Democrat Al Gore

Table 4.4	The break-up of the 'solid South', 1992–2006		

Year	House: Democrats–Republicans	Senate: Democrats–Republicans	Governors: Democrats–Republicans
1992	77–48	13–9	8–3
1994	61–64	9–13	5–6
1996	54–71	7–15	5–6
1998	54–71	8–14	4–7
2000	53–71	9–13	5–6
2002	55–76	9–13	4–7
2004	49–82	4–18	4–7
2006	54–77	5–17	5–6

The break-up of the 'solid South' has been brought about by mainly white, conservative voters in the South switching to the Republican Party. These white southerners had voted Democrat for a century following the Civil War (1861–65) in a practice known as 'vote as you shot'. But the years between 1960 and 1988 saw the Democratic Party field a number of presidential candidates who were far too liberal — and maybe too 'northern' — to appeal to these southern, conservative voters. Candidates such as John F. Kennedy (1960), Hubert Humphrey (1968), George McGovern (1972), Walter Mondale (1984) and Michael Dukakis (1988) had huge difficulty attracting votes in the South. And this was at a time when the South, because its population was growing faster than in other areas of America, was gaining in political importance. More people meant more members in the House of Representatives and more Electoral College votes.

Republican Presidents Richard Nixon (1969–74) and Ronald Reagan (1981–89) went out of their way to court southern, conservative voters. Nixon had his 'southern strategy'. During the 1980s, there were the 'Reagan Democrats'. Even some politicians switched parties — Senators Strom Thurmond of South Carolina and Phil Gramm of Texas both began their political careers as Democrats but ended them as Republicans. Both were from the South. Other southern conservative Democrats merely retired, usually to be replaced by Republicans.

With southern conservative voters leaving the old 'New Deal coalition' — northeastern liberals plus southern conservatives — that had kept the Democrats as the majority party for half a century, the Democrats were left as a more homogenously liberal party. True, Bill Clinton (1993–2001) tried to move the party somewhat more to the centre — the so-called 'New Democrats'

— but his impact was limited both in terms of degree and durability. With the arrival of the southern conservatives, the Republican Party became a more homogenously conservative party. Indeed, the Democrats found it increasingly difficult to hold on to their open Senate seats in the South, as Table 4.5 shows. In 2004, the Democrats lost all 5 of their open Senate seats to the Republicans — in Florida, Georgia and Louisiana, as well as in North and South Carolina.

Table 4.5 Open southern Senate seats lost by the Democratic Party, 1993–2004

Year	Senator retiring	State	Party	Replaced by	Party
1993	Lloyd Bentsen	Texas	D	Kay Bailey Hutchison	R
1996	Howell Heflin	Alabama	D	Jeff Sessions	R
1996	David Pryor	Arkansas	D	Tim Hutchinson	R
2004	Bob Graham	Florida	D	Mel Martinez	R
2004	Zell Miller	Georgia	D	Johnny Isakson	R
2004	John Breaux	Louisiana	D	David Vitter	R
2004	John Edwards	North Carolina	D	Richard Burr	R
2004	Ernest Hollings	South Carolina	D	Jim DeMint	R

If the parties are more ideologically homogenous, then it is not surprising that they tend to vote together more often, and more consistently vote against the other side. Bipartisanship is more difficult. In the 1980s, Republican President Reagan could get some of his more conservative policies through a Democrat-controlled House of Representatives by appealing to southern conservative Democrats, such as Charles Bennett of Florida. Here is Reagan biographer Dinesh D'Souza writing about the passage of Reagan's tax cut in 1981 (from *Ronald Reagan: How an Ordinary Man Became an Extraordinary Leader*):

> Congress approved, and Reagan signed into law the central plank of Reagan's campaign platform: the largest tax cut in American history. The vote was relatively close in the House of Representatives, 238 to 195, yet several conservative Democrats had defected from their party to vote with the President.

Were George W. Bush to face a similar political scenario, he would find life much more difficult. There just aren't that many southern conservative Democrats left to whom to appeal.

(2) The election of 'divisive' presidents

On the night in November 1968 when he was declared winner of the presidential election, Richard Nixon spoke to a group of reporters:

I saw many signs in this campaign. Some of them were not friendly, and some were very friendly. But the one that touched me the most was the one I saw in Deshler, Ohio, at the end of a long day of whistle-stopping. A little town, I suppose five times the population was there in the dusk, almost impossible to see — but a teenager held up a sign, 'Bring Us Together'. And that will be the great objective of this administration at the outset, to bring the American people together.

Few believed that Nixon achieved much 'togetherness' during his tumultuous presidency.

Governor George W. Bush, running for the presidency in 2000, frequently described himself as 'a uniter, not a divider'. By this he hoped to distinguish himself from President Clinton, who was generally agreed to have been a divisive president. Ironically, at the time of writing, George W. Bush has proved to be just as divisive — some might say more so — as his predecessor. This means that for a 16-year period American politics has been dominated by divisive presidents. Clinton and George W. Bush are, in this sense, quite unlike other modern-day presidents — Ford, Carter or George Bush. These three presidents were, I would argue, less divisive characters. You don't have to rate them — or their policies — highly to agree with that claim. Few people 'loved' or 'hated' these presidents. As a general rule, these three were more modest, quiet men who were happy to do deals and make compromises.

In contrast, Clinton and George W. Bush appear more similar to Presidents Lyndon Johnson (1963–69) and Richard Nixon (1969–74) — presidents about whom it was almost impossible to have lukewarm views. You were either an ardent admirer or a fervent hater. To some, LBJ was the saviour of America's inner cities and the mover behind much-needed civil rights reforms. To others, it was 'Hey, hey, LBJ, how many kids have you killed today?' They hated him for the war in Vietnam. Nixon's admirers extolled his brilliance in foreign policy — in the Middle East, China, and détente with the Soviet Union. To others, Nixon was nothing more than a crook. In 1960, a Democrat poster had shown Nixon's face with the caption: 'Would you buy a second-hand car from this man?' (The Democrats re-ran the poster in 1972, changing it to read: 'Would you buy a second-hand war from this man?')

If there were few neutrals when it came to either Johnson or Nixon, then the same can be said of Clinton and George W. Bush. To some, Clinton was a Democrat poster boy — the first Democrat to serve two full terms since Franklin D. Roosevelt. To others, he was an ill-disciplined, womanising wide-boy who would lie his way out of anything. George W. Bush's admirers extol his gritty determination and his moral values, seeing him as someone who has — as promised — restored dignity to the Oval Office. To others, George W. Bush was an illegitimate president in his first term, and merely an incompetent one in his second.

An anti-Vietnam war rally, 1968

The result, some argue, is a divided, partisan country — one that is split into blue (Democrat) states and red (Republican) states. These divisive characteristics tend to show themselves in the views of many ordinary American voters, as a recent *Washington Post* article showed only too well. It quoted Britton Stein of Sugar Land, Texas (Red America), describing George W. Bush as 'a man's man, a manly man,' while Al Gore was 'a ranting and raving little whiny baby'. On the other hand, Tom Harrison of San Francisco (Blue America) described Bill Clinton as 'intelligent', 'charismatic', and 'a good representation of America'. According to Harrison, George W. Bush is 'frightening', 'a total imbecile' and a 'monkey boy'.

Of course, such comments are dreadful caricatures of American politics, but like most caricatures they contain an element of recognisable truth. We must hardly be surprised if a Congress elected in such times and by such voters is more deeply divided and partisan than those of times gone by.

Task 4.1

Study the figures in Tables 4.1 and 4.2 on party unity in Congress between 1981 and 2006. How do they show that party unity has increased in Congress in the last 25 years?

Guidance

The key is to look for the highest figures in each column. These are shown in bold. You could also identify in which years the lowest figures were recorded.

Task 4.2

(a) What do you understand by the term 'the solid South' as it was traditionally used?

(b) What does Table 4.4 tell you about the strength of the two major parties in the South between 1992 and 2006?

Guidance

(a) You need to correctly identify which party won most elections in the South for more than a century following the Civil War of the 1860s. You can get some idea of how the South traditionally voted in presidential elections by visiting **www.uselectionatlas.org**.

Task 4.3

Using the contents of this chapter and any other information you have, write a short essay (approximately 300–400 words) in answer to this question:

Analyse the main reasons why Congress has become more partisan.

Guidance

(a) Try to define the word 'partisan' or 'partisanship'.

(b) Briefly consider the evidence for increased partisanship in Congress.

(c) Consider the reasons for this increased partisanship.

(d) Is there any evidence to the contrary — that Congress is in fact *not* necessarily becoming more partisan?

Further reading

- Princeton University Conference, *The Polarization of American Politics: Myth or Reality?* 3–4 December 2004. Available on the internet from www.princeton.edu — type the title of the conference into the search box.

Better to be a Senator than a House member?

To answer this question we will need to consider a number of different pieces of evidence, including the career paths of House and Senate members, as well as their terms of office and the exclusive and concurrent powers of both houses. Some evidence will point to one answer; other evidence will suggest something different. We shall see in the end that there are arguments on both sides.

Better to be a Senator

Career paths

If one looks at the career paths of members of the House and the Senate, it soon becomes obvious that the traffic is one-way. While many House members aspire to become Senators, no Senator aspires to membership of the House. Republican Senator Trent Lott of Mississippi and Democrat Senator Charles Schumer of New York don't have much in common, but one thing they do share is that they — along with 48 other Senators — are former members of the House of Representatives.

The only House member in recent years to have previously held a Senate seat was Democrat Claude Pepper of Florida. When Pepper died on 30 May 1989, aged 88, he was the oldest member of Congress. He had been elected to represent Florida in the Senate in 1937 and served there for 14 years, before being defeated for a third full term in 1950. Undaunted by his Senate defeat, at the age of 62 he ran for a House seat in 1962 and represented Florida's 18th District for the next 27 years. But it should be noted that he settled for a House seat only after losing his seat in the Senate.

Whereas House members will often aspire to the Senate, Senators often aspire to the governorships of large states, to the vice-presidency, or even to the presidency. In 2005, Democrat Senator Jon Corzine of New Jersey was elected governor of his state. Three of the last vice-presidents — Walter Mondale (1977–81), Dan Quayle (1989–93) and Al Gore (1993–2001) — were serving members of the Senate when elected to office. And in 2004, the Democratic candidates for both president and vice-president — John Kerry of Massachusetts and John Edwards of North Carolina — were serving Senators. That year's Democratic presidential primaries saw not only Senators Kerry and Edwards in the nomination race, but also Senators Joe Lieberman of Connecticut, Bob Graham of Florida, and former Senator Carol Moseley Braun of Illinois. Four of the five presidents who served between 1945 and 1969 were Senators — Harry S. Truman, John F. Kennedy, Lyndon Johnson and Richard Nixon.

In contrast, no serving member of the House of Representatives has been chosen as a presidential candidate for either the Democratic or the Republican Party. In 1984, Representative Geraldine Ferraro, a three-term congresswoman from New York, was nominated as the Democratic Party's vice-presidential candidate. The Mondale-Ferraro ticket won just one state. Thus the career paths of Senators and House members seem to suggest a positive answer to the question posed by this chapter.

Terms of office and representation

The House and the Senate pose quite a contrast regarding their terms of office. Whereas House members must seek re-election every 2 years, Senators serve 6-year terms. Robert Byrd, a Democrat from West Virginia, was first elected to the Senate in 1958. He's still there, but in 2006 he fought only his ninth election. Cliff Stearns, a Republican from Florida, was also fighting his ninth election in 2006 — but to the House of Representatives. Stearns was first elected only in 1988.

Another important difference between House and Senate members is *who* they represent. Whereas most House members represent only part of their state — a congressional district — Senators represent the entire state. Thus, in Florida, Cliff Stearns represents the 6th congressional district, an area of some 3,000 square miles in north-central Florida, around the city of Gainesville, with a population of around 640,000. But the two Senators from Florida — Democrat Bill Nelson and Republican Mel Martinez — both represent the entire state, all 16 million Floridians spread across 66,000 square miles. Not only does this make Senators more important than House members, it also brings them state-wide name recognition — which, especially in large population states, can often bring national name recognition.

In terms of numbers, a Senator is 1 of 100. A House member is 1 of 435. To get things done in the Senate, you need just 50 allies. In the House you need 217. Because there are virtually the same number of leadership positions in both houses, one is far more likely to pick up a leadership position as a Senator than as a House member. In 2006, all 55 Republican Senators held either a post in

the party leadership or were a committee or subcommittee chair. Indeed, many held 2 and some 3 such positions. Kay Bailey Hutchison of Texas was Republican Party Conference Vice-Chair, as well as holding the chair of two subcommittees. Saxby Chambliss made it to chair of the standing committee on Agriculture, Nutrition and Forestry just 4 years after his election to the Senate. By contrast, House Republican Howard Coble of North Carolina has yet to gain a committee chair in the House, despite having served there since 1984. He currently ranks only number 2 in seniority on the House Judiciary Committee, and number 4 on the committee for Transportation and Infrastructure. Better, indeed, to be a Senator than a House member.

Kay Bailey Hutchison

Exclusive powers

Both the House of Representatives and the Senate are given exclusive powers by Articles I and II of the Constitution. However, those given to the Senate are more significant than those given to the House. In Article II, the Constitution states that:

> [The president] shall have power, *by and with the advice and consent of the Senate*, to make treaties, provided that two-thirds of the Senators present concur; and he shall nominate, and *by and with the advice and consent of the Senate*, shall appoint ambassadors, other public ministers and consuls, judges of the Supreme Court, and all other officers of the United States whose appointments are herein provided for and which shall be established by law.

This gives the Senate two important powers concerning the confirmation of appointments — both executive and judicial — and the ratification of treaties.

Confirmation of appointments

The president gets to make hundreds of appointments each year to the executive and judicial branches of the federal government. The Senate has to decide whether to confirm or reject most of those to the executive branch and all of those to the judiciary. It therefore has the power to confirm or reject literally hundreds of executive and judicial branch appointments every year. In 2006, George W. Bush needed votes to confirm a number of high profile members of the executive branch, including Dirk Kempthorne to be Secretary of the Interior. Governor Kempthorne of Idaho was confirmed by the Senate on 26 May, by a recorded vote of 85–8.

Note that the Senate does not have power over most of the appointments within the Executive Office of the President, the assumption being that as these are the president's personal aides and advisers, he may appoint whomever he wishes. One exception to this is the Director of the Office of Management and Budget (OMB), who is subject to Senate confirmation given his/her significant powers over the drafting of the federal budget. So when Jim Nussle was nominated by President George W. Bush to be OMB Director in June 2007, the Senate had to vote on whether or not to confirm him.

Admittedly it is highly unusual for the Senate to defeat or block an executive branch nomination, although a Republican-controlled Senate blocked the nomination of John Bolton as US Ambassador to the United Nations after a prolonged filibuster by Democrats, joined by Ohio Republican George Voinovich. Eventually, the President appointed Bolton as a recess appointment on 1 August 2005, meaning that he could hold office until the end of the 109th Congress in January 2007. In 1989, a Democrat-controlled Senate rejected Republican President George Bush's choice of John Tower to be Secretary of Defense.

However, the Senate has confirmation power over all the president's nominations to the federal judiciary. The ones that get publicised are those to the Supreme Court, but a president can expect to make around 60 nominations a year to the federal judiciary, as Table 5.1 shows. During his first term, George W. Bush made no nominations to the Supreme Court but did get to make 268 nominations to the lower federal courts, of which the Senate confirmed 216.

Table 5.1 **Judicial nominations and confirmations, 2001–06**

Years	Judicial nominations by the President	Number confirmed by the Senate
2001–02	131	100
2003–04	137	116
2005–06	97	54
Totals	**365**	**270**

Recent years have seen the blocking of some judicial nominations in the Senate through the use of the filibuster. This came to a head during the presidency of

George W. Bush when the Democrat minority in the Senate used the filibuster tactic to block the confirmation of judges it regarded as too conservative. This brought a threat from the then Majority Leader Bill Frist that he would introduce 'the nuclear option' — in other words, change the Senate rules to stop filibusters against judicial nominations.

Following this threat, however, a group of 14 moderate Senators — 7 Democrats and 7 Republicans — reached a compromise that averted a crisis on the issue. The 'gang of 14' agreed that a filibuster would in future be used only in 'extraordinary circumstances'.

Ratification of treaties

Another exclusive power of the Senate is the ratification of treaties. While it is the president — or, more realistically, those working on his behalf — who negotiates treaties with foreign powers, these become operational only following ratification by a two-thirds majority of the Senate. As with appointments, rejections are unusual. But then presidents will tend to negotiate only those treaties of which they are fairly confident of receiving Senate ratification. It is also possible for a president simply not to submit a treaty to the Senate, leaving it in limbo rather than risking defeat. Hence, Carter never presented his Salt 2 treaty for Senate ratification. Neither did Clinton or George W. Bush present the Kyoto Treaty on climate change. Both would have been defeated.

During the twentieth century, the Senate defeated only 7 treaties, of which just 2 — the Treaty of Versailles (1920) and the Comprehensive Test Ban Treaty (1999) — were genuinely high profile agreements. They served as significant political defeats respectively for presidents Woodrow Wilson and Bill Clinton. Both presidents were coming to the end of their second term, and were Democrats facing a Senate controlled by the Republican Party. Wilson was a sick man, having just suffered a heart attack. Clinton was politically weakened by impeachment.

Just as recess appointments provide a president with a way round the Senate check of confirmation of appointments, so executive agreements can provide a way round the ratification of treaties. Such agreements do not require Senate ratification and are made under the president's power as commander-in-chief. The Supreme Court bolstered their use through its decision in *United States* v *Belmont* (1937), in which it declared that executive agreements are legally equal to treaties and thus enjoy the status of 'supreme law of the land'. They enable the president to take quick and decisive action in a crisis. But over-use of executive agreements by presidents Franklin D. Roosevelt, Harry S. Truman and Dwight Eisenhower led in the 1950s to the introduction of a constitutional amendment which would have required such agreements also to receive Senate ratification — the so-called Bricker Amendment, named after its sponsor Senator John Bricker of Ohio. The amendment failed to achieve a two-thirds vote in the Senate by just one vote. But it was a warning shot across the presidential bows.

Congress again acted against executive agreements in the 1970s with the Case Act (1972), which required that presidents inform Congress of all executive agreements that they negotiate. The Case Act was a reaction to President Nixon making secret executive agreements.

Despite the possibility of bypassing them, these two exclusive powers of the Senate remain important and go a long way towards accounting for why politicians would rather be a Senator than a member of the House of Representatives.

Summary

Thus we see that Senators have numerous advantages over House members:
- They are far more likely to be regarded as potential presidential (or vice-presidential) candidates than House members.
- They serve 6-year terms as opposed to 2-year terms in the House.
- They represent the entire state rather than just a part of that state.
- There are fewer of them — 100 Senators compared with 435 House members.
- They are more likely to hold leadership positions.
- They enjoy exclusive powers to confirm appointments and ratify treaties.

The counter-argument

All these points are valid and important, but they are not the whole story. There are some ways in which members of the Senate and House are equal, and it makes no difference at all whether you are a Senator or a House member. There are principally four ways in which this is the case:
- in the introduction, consideration and passage of legislation
- in the scrutiny and investigation of the executive branch
- in the initiation of constitutional amendments
- in salaries

(1) Introduction, consideration and passage of legislation

It is easy to forget that with regard to the principal function of Congress — its legislative function — both the House and the Senate are equal. Indeed, in terms of the introduction of legislation, it is the House of Representatives that might be regarded as slightly more important than the Senate, since all money bills must be first introduced in the House of Representatives. This was mandated

by the framers of the Constitution, because at the time the House was the only directly elected chamber. Thus they believed that, when spending the people's money, the people's directly elected representatives should have the first say. However, once the Senate also became directly elected, in 1914, the reason for this provision was negated. Neither does this power of the House have the same level of exclusivity that the Senate's powers have over the confirmation of appointments and the ratification of treaties. Money bills merely *begin* in the House. They must also be fully considered by the Senate. The House has no power at all over the confirmation of appointments or the ratification of treaties.

Yet in every other respect, in terms of legislation the Senate and the House are equal. All legislation must pass through all stages in both houses. The legislative process in both houses is pretty much identical: first reading; committee stage; second reading; third reading. In both houses there is therefore a series of floor debates and committee hearings. Both houses have a set of policy-specialist standing committees that consider the bill at the committee stage. There is a House Agriculture Committee and a Senate Agriculture Committee, for example. Bills are usually considered by the two houses concurrently, rather than consecutively as occurs in the UK parliament. At the end of the third reading in each chamber, there are therefore usually two versions of the same bill — the House version and the Senate version — and these may differ fundamentally. Of course, only one version of a bill can be passed to the president for his signature, which must have been agreed by both chambers. Thus the need for a conference committee on many bills. The job of the conference committee is to reconcile the differences between the two versions of the same bill in a way that is acceptable to both chambers.

At the conference committee stage of the legislative process, the equality of the two chambers is again on display. The conference committee is made up of members of both chambers. The version of a bill decided upon by the conference committee must then be agreed to by a simple majority of both chambers. Whereas in the UK parliament, the House of Commons — through the provisions of the Parliament Act — holds the upper hand at this stage of the legislative process, in the US Congress both chambers must sign up to the final version of the bill. Only then can the bill be sent to the president for his approval or veto.

Should the president choose to veto a bill, his veto can be overridden only by a two-thirds majority vote in both houses. In October 1997, President Clinton vetoed the Late-Term Abortion Ban Bill. The House voted to override the President's veto by 296 votes to 132 — 11 votes over the 285 votes required for a two-thirds majority. But the vote in the Senate was 64–36, 3 votes short of the required two-thirds majority. The President's veto was therefore sustained.

In terms of legislation therefore, there is little difference at all in being a Senator rather than a House member.

(2) Scrutiny and investigation of the executive branch

Both chambers play an important role in the scrutiny and investigation of the executive branch. This function is carried out largely by the congressional standing committees. With a strict separation of personnel between the legislature and the executive, it is not possible for Congress to conduct an equivalent of the Question Time that occurs in the UK parliament. Members of the executive branch are simply not present in either chamber of Congress to answer the questions. It is only in the committee rooms that this role can be carried out in Congress.

(3) Initiating constitutional amendments

When it comes to Congress's power to initiate constitutional amendments, it is much the same story of bicameral equality. Both chambers must approve the amendment by a two-thirds majority. There have been two examples in recent years where the House of Representatives has approved a constitutional amendment but the Senate has not. The first was in January 1995, when the House approved a constitutional amendment requiring the federal government to have a balanced budget. The vote was 300–132, 12 votes over the 288 votes required for the two-thirds majority. But when the Senate came to vote on the same amendment in March, the vote (65–35) fell just 2 short of the two-thirds majority. There was to be no balanced budget amendment.

The second example was when the House voted on four occasions between 1995 and 2006 for a constitutional amendment banning the desecration of the American flag. On all four occasions, the vote received the required two-thirds majority. But the Senate has consistently refused to pass the amendment. In the three votes it has had on the amendment during this period, the votes have always fallen just short of the two-thirds hurdle — in 2006, by just one vote (see Table 5.2).

Table 5.2 **House and Senate votes on constitutional amendment to ban the desecration of the American flag, 1995–2006**

Years (Congress)	House vote	Senate vote
1995–96 (104th)	312–120	62–36
1997–98 (105th)	310–114	Did not vote
1999–2000 (106th)	305–124	63-37
2005–06 (109th)	286–130	66-34

(4) Salaries

Finally, there is one tangible way in which there is no difference at all between being a Senator and a member of the House of Representatives. This is in the matter of their salaries. As of October 2006, the members of both chambers received an annual salary of $165,200.

Conclusion

So, better to be a Senator than a member of the House of Representatives? I guess most, if not all, of those 50 Senators who are former members of the House would answer in the affirmative. So would those who have used the Senate as a stepping-stone to higher office — vice presidents Walter Mondale, Dan Quayle and Al Gore, for example. Certainly, the field of presidential candidates is still dominated by serving or former members of the Senate — John Kerry, John Edwards, John McCain and Hillary Clinton, to name but a few. But the Senate can be a frustrating place in which to work. With its archaic rules and filibustering, its idiosyncratic members like Robert Byrd of West Virginia, its cumbersome way of doing business — or of not doing business — it can be the graveyard of legislative action and political ambition. But for all that, and for all the counter-arguments, the answer is probably 'yes'.

Task 5.1

Using the contents of this chapter and any other information you have, write a short essay (approximately 300–400 words) in answer to the question:

Is it better to be a Senator than a House member?

Guidance

(a) Establish how many Senators are former House members. You can work this out from the information in the second paragraph of this chapter. There are currently no House members who are former Senators.

(b) Discuss the advantages that being a Senator has over being a House member. They concern both terms of office and powers.

(c) Briefly consider the arguments against the proposition.

What's wrong with Congress?

I'm rather fond of quoting to my classes the American bumper sticker I once saw which read: 'What's the opposite of progress? Congress!' It seems to sum up what many Americans feel about their legislative branch of government. Even in the scholarly world, one has only to scan the bibliographies of books about Congress to see that the titles are often unflattering: *Congress and the Decline of Public Trust* (Westview, 1999) or *Congress as Public Enemy* (Cambridge University Press, 1995). There is plenty of evidence that Congress is generally a pretty unpopular institution in the United States. So why is this? What *is* wrong with Congress?

Evidence that something is wrong

The evidence that there is something wrong with Congress comes in the form of polling data. In March 2007, three polling organisations asked the question, 'Do you approve or disapprove of the way Congress is handling its job?' The average approval rating was just 32%. The average disapproval rating was 56%. Even President George W. Bush — not the most popular politician of his day — had a higher approval rating. Neither was 'disapproval' limited to Republicans disgruntled at the takeover of Congress by the Democrats the previous January. In the CBS News/*New York Times* poll, only 34% of Democrats said that they approved of the way Congress was handling its job, while 47% of Democrats disapproved.

As can be seen from Table 6.1, these were not the worst approval figures that Congress had received in recent years. The same CBS poll back in May 2006 had found a 23% approval and 64% disapproval rating for Congress. Nor were these figures a temporary blip. The CBS poll has registered an approval rating for Congress of over 50% on only two occasions over the last 8 years: a 67% approval rating in October 2001 and a 57% approval rating in December of the same year. But these were the first two sets of data available following the attacks on the United States on 11 September 2001. You will remember that President Bush's approval rating likewise soared immediately following these events. Congress's ratings quickly slumped and by June 2002 were back to 43%.

Table 6.1			

Congressional job ratings, August 2001–March 2007

Date	Approve (%)	Disapprove (%)	Unsure (%)
7–11 March 2007	31	53	16
23–27 February 2007	33	50	17
18–21 January 2007	33	49	18
27–31 October 2006	29	56	15
15–19 September 2006	25	61	14
17–21 August 2006	29	60	11
21–25 July 2006	28	58	14
10–11 June 2006	26	60	14
4–8 May 2006	23	64	13
6–9 April 2006	27	61	12
9–12 March 2006	32	54	14
22–26 February 2006	28	61	11
5–8 January 2006	17	57	16
2–6 December 2005	33	53	14
3–5 October 2005	31	57	12
9–13 September 2005	34	54	12
13–14 July 2005	33	50	17
10–15 June 2005	33	53	14
20–23 May 2005	29	55	16
13–16 April 2005	35	51	14
21–22 March 2005	34	49	17
24–28 February 2005	41	44	15
14–18 January 2005	44	39	17
14–17 October 2004	38	46	16
12–15 January 2004	45	42	13
28–30 September 2003	37	47	16
9–12 May 2003	35	48	17
2–4 November 2002	42	45	13
16–18 June 2002	43	40	17
24–26 February 2002	50	34	16
21–24 January 2002	47	37	14
7–10 December 2001	57	31	12
25–28 October 2001	67	24	9
28–31 August 2001	43	41	16

Source: CBS News/*New York Times* poll (www.pollingreport.com)

The trouble is that while there is plenty of evidence that Americans hold Congress as an institution in low esteem, there is equally plenty of evidence that they hold their own Senators and House members in high esteem. The most obvious proof for this is the high rate of re-election in both the Senate and the House of Representatives. As Table 6.1 shows, in October 2006 Congress's approval rating was just 29%. Yet in the mid-term House and Senate elections the following week, 79% of Senators and 94% of House members who sought re-election succeeded. In the House, this meant that of the 403 incumbents contesting the elections, only 22 were defeated.

So, if they are dissatisfied with Congress, why do Americans keep re-electing their members? The simple answer is that while a high percentage of Americans consistently say that they disapprove of Congress as an institution, most are not dissatisfied with their own Senators and House member. Or to put it another way, their motto for congressional elections might be summed up as: 'Throw the bums out — but my Congressman isn't a bum!' Indeed, many members of Congress get re-elected by running *against* Congress. That wouldn't have been too difficult if you were a Democrat between 1995 and 2006, because you could run against the *Republican-controlled* Congress. But members of Congress manage to do this even if they are in the majority party, and sometimes even if they are members of the majority party leadership.

Members of Congress are also good at criticising other members of Congress while doing similar things themselves. A member of Congress might criticise 'wasteful pork barrel spending' by Congress and yet boast that 'I fight to get a fair share of federal spending' for his own state or district. A congressman representing a rural district will proudly proclaim that he 'fights to protect family farmers' but criticise steel subsidies. A congressman representing a steel-producing district is proud of steel subsidies but will criticise Congress for 'wasteful farm subsidies', and so on. As a result, some of the harshest criticism of Congress comes from Congress itself. Take this statement from Congressman Ron Paul (Republican–Texas) in 2004 on the subject of Congress's oversight of the Iraq War — and Paul was a member of the majority party:

> Congress is to blame for its craven failure to seriously debate, much less declare, war in Iraq. The Constitution squarely charges Congress with the duty to declare war. A proper investigation and debate by Congress clearly was warranted *before* any decision to go to war. The current after-the-fact debate is hollow and political. We now see those who abdicated their congressional responsibility to declare or reject war, who timidly voted to give the President the power he wanted, posturing as his harshest critics.

We can identify eight factors that are wrong with Congress and are worthy of examination:

- gerrymandering of House districts
- growth of ideological polarisation
- term limits for committee chairs
- diffusion of power in Congress
- ethical problems
- 3-day working week
- senate's abuse of the filibuster
- ineffective oversight of the executive branch

In the remainder of this chapter, we shall consider each of these matters in turn.

(1) Gerrymandering of House districts

First, we need an explanation of the term. 'Gerrymandering' originates in early nineteenth-century American political history. It is said to have been coined in 1812, when a cartoonist drew a picture of a sprawling electoral district in Massachusetts, which he made resemble a salamander with claws, wings and teeth. The Governor of Massachusetts at the time, who was behind the drawing up of the district, was one Elbridge Gerry. The editor in whose newspaper the cartoon appeared came up with the title of the 'gerrymander' to refer to an electoral district drawn up for the political benefit of one party.

THE GERRY-MANDER.

Corbis

America holds a 10-yearly census in each year divisible by 10 — 1980, 1990, 2000 etc. After each census, the 435 seats in the House of Representatives are reallocated, with some states gaining and others losing one or more seats. Any state which has its allocation of House seats changed must redraw the state's congressional district boundaries. But unlike in the UK, where this is done by a non-partisan body, in the US the redrawing of House seats is done by the state legislature which, of course, is under the political control of one party. Recent redrawing of congressional district boundaries has resulted in a significant increase in gerrymandering, by which either the Democrats or Republicans have sought to redraw the boundaries to their electoral advantage.

Nowhere has this been seen more clearly than in Texas following the 2000 census. After that census, the Democrats controlled the state legislature. But in 2002, the Republicans won control from the Democrats. At the urging of the then US House Majority Leader Tom DeLay, the Texas Republicans proposed another redrawing of the congressional district boundaries to increase the likelihood of the Republicans gaining House seats in 2004. The effect was to give a number of Democrat House members either unfamiliar and more conservative districts; to combine their districts, thus pitting two incumbent Democrats against each other; or to pit them against a Republican incumbent in an overwhelmingly Republican district. The Democrats in the Texas state legislature tried every possible device to thwart the Republicans' plan. They even fled the state en masse on two occasions — once to Oklahoma and once to New Mexico — to try to prevent the Republicans from obtaining a quorum and to avoid arrest under an obscure Texas state law aimed at preventing such a tactic. Eventually, after months of wrangling, the Republicans won.

The effect of this redistricting was remarkable. After the 2002 House elections, the Republicans held 15 of the state's 32 House seats. But after the Republicans' gerrymandered districts came into force, one House Democrat (Ralph Hall) defected to the Republicans; another retired; another was defeated in a primary; and four were defeated in the House elections of 2004. After the 2004 elections, the Republicans had increased their share of the Texas House delegation from 15 seats to 21. In the other 49 states, the Republicans suffered a net loss of 3 seats. But the gerrymandering of Texas meant that the Republicans gained seats in the House overall in this election. (For more on the Texas redistricting, see Gary C. Jacobsen's 'The Congress: The structural basis of Republican success' in Michael Nelson (ed.), *The Elections of 2004*, CQ Press, 2005.)

Through the 10-yearly redistricting, there has also been a significant decline in competitive seats in elections for the House of Representatives. For example, of the 25 districts that the Republicans won with less than 55% of the vote in 2000 (before the last redistricting), 18 were made more Republican by

increasing the proportion of 2000 Bush voters. Of the 19 similarly marginal Democratic districts, 15 were made more Democratic by increasing the proportion of 2000 Gore voters. The decline in competitive House seats between 1992 and 2004 can be clearly seen in Table 6.2. This is deeply worrying. If only 30-odd seats — out of 435 — are viewed as competitive in an election, it seriously calls into question the accountability of the institution itself. It may also be a contributory factor to low levels of turnout in congressional races.

Table 6.2 **Number of competitive House districts, 1992–2004**

Year	Number of competitive House districts
1992	103
1994	98
1996	104
1998	58
2000	53
2002	47
2004	37

The lack of competitive seats may also contribute to what some perceive as rising levels of partisanship in American politics. Samuel Isaacharoff, a professor at Columbia Law School, states: 'Partisan gerrymandering skews not only the positions congressmen take but also who the candidates are in the first place.' Isaacharoff points out that you are likely to get more partisan candidates when you don't have to worry about the electability of the candidate or appealing to independent voters. As a result of redistricting, conservative Democrats like Charles Stenholm of Texas, who reached out across party lines, have been replaced by reliable Republicans who have no need to compromise across the aisle. In the same way, moderate Republicans like Jim Leach of Iowa have been replaced by reliable Democrats.

In the view of David Skaggs, who was a Democrat House member from Colorado between 1987 and 1999, because 'more members are coming out of safe seats, they are less trained to listen and to accommodate.'

(2) Growth of ideological polarisation

There has been much comment of late about America having become a '50/50 nation', divided into red states (Republican) and blue states (Democrat). Partisanship in Congress has increased. In 1970, Republican House members voted with a majority of their fellow Republicans on only 60% of votes.

In 2003, the figure was 91%. In 1970, Democrat House members voted with a majority of their fellow Democrats only 58% of votes. In 2005, the figure was 88%.

Writing at the end of the 109th Congress in December 2006, Jonathan Allen of *Congressional Quarterly* commented that the voting patterns in Congress during 2006 'reveal a Congress that remained as sharply polarised as it had been for more than a decade.' In the House, the share of the roll call votes that pitted the majority of Republicans against the majority of Democrats rose to almost 55%, the highest since 1998. In the Senate, the figure was 57% — the highest in an election year since 1996. Polarisation is seen too in the increase in unanimous voting in both chambers. Back in 1992, there were only 87 occasions when Republicans or Democrats in either chamber voted unanimously. By 1995, the figure had risen to 343, and by 2003 it was up to 365.

The 110th Congress, which began work in January 2007, was missing a number of conservative Democrats and moderate Republicans who had either retired or been defeated in the 2006 mid-term elections. Of the 3 most moderate Republicans whose seats were up for re-election in 2006, 2 of them — Lincoln Chafee of Rhode Island and Mike DeWine of Ohio — were defeated. The most moderate Republican in the House — Jim Leach of Iowa — lost his re-election bid in the same election. Of the 21 House Republicans who lost on Election Day in 2006, 6 were among the party's most moderate members, including Rob Simmons of Connecticut (5th most moderate), Mike Fitzpatrick of Pennsylvania (8th most moderate) and Nancy Johnson of Connecticut (11th most moderate).

Moreover, the Senate has in recent years lost conservative Democrats such as John Breaux of Louisiana and Zell Miller of Georgia. Breaux was replaced by Republican David Vitter, who in 2006 was ranked by *National Journal* as the 12th most conservative member of the Senate. Miller was replaced by Republican Johnny Isakson, who in 2006 was ranked as the 6th most conservative member. Here, then, are two examples where moderately conservative Democrats have been replaced by highly partisan Republicans. The same was true in reverse of the Ohio Senate seat in 2006 where moderate Republican Mike DeWine was defeated by liberal Democrat House member Sherrod Brown.

Both the Senate and House chambers are set out so that members sit in a large semicircle. The semicircle is divided by a central aisle, with Republicans to the left and Democrats to the right — as viewed from the presiding officer's chair. There's a much-used phrase in American politics about members of both sides 'reaching across the aisle' — meaning that they are happy from time to time to work and even vote with those who sit on the other side, so that moderate Republicans work with Democrats and conservative Democrats work with

Republicans. This is how the work of Congress has traditionally been advanced — through bipartisanship, negotiation and compromise. Most votes in Congress were traditionally one group of Democrats and Republicans voting against another group of Democrats and Republicans. That is how politics worked during lengthy periods of divided government, when the president was from one party and Congress was controlled by the other. The alternative is gridlock. Today, in Congress, there is less 'reaching across the aisle', less bipartisanship.

(3) Term limits for committee chairs

While Congress has spurned most major reforms during recent decades, it has indulged in tinkering. One example of this was the introduction of term limits for chairs of standing committees introduced when the Republicans took control of Congress in 1995. The new rule was that chairs of standing committees could hold their position for only 6 years. The House Republicans began the clock ticking on the term limits straight away in January 1995; the Senate Republicans followed 2 years later.

Admittedly, the old system under which chairs held on to their posts for decades — and well past their 'best by' date — was heavily and rightly criticised. The Republicans had done a lot of this criticising during the 40-year period (1955–94) in which the Democrats had control of the House of Representatives. So when they took over the helm, they swept away the so-called 'seniority rule' — what critics called 'the senility rule' — by which the chair of a standing committee was automatically the member of the majority party who had the longest continuous service on that committee.

But as a result of these new term limit rules, by January 2001, 14 of the 18 House standing committee chairs had reached their 6-year limit and therefore had to be replaced. Major committees such as the House Armed Services Committee, the House Judiciary Committee and the House Ways and Means Committee all had to have new chairs. Many thought this a mistake. First, the institutional memory of the committee, which was nurtured by long-serving chairs, would be lost. Moreover, a new chair is likely to rely more heavily on unelected and unaccountable committee staffers. Second, it introduced intra-party squabbles among committee members for the chairs of committees. Some even started campaigning for chairs among their House party colleagues. Third, it made the president's job more difficult in negotiating and working with Congress. Under the seniority rule, presidents knew with whom they would be doing business in Congress in any particular policy area. Now the matter was much more unpredictable and fluid. As former Congressman David Skaggs (Democrat–Colorado) has commented:

When chairmanships were awarded by seniority, everyone knew where he or she stood. Now ambitious members angling for a chair must prove themselves to the party.

In the Senate, the term limits clock did not start until January 1997. But by June 2001, the Republicans had reverted to the minority party, so no Senate chair completed his 6-year term. When the Republicans regained the majority in January 2003, the clock was restarted at zero, as it were. Four years later, the Republicans were back in the minority again. So term limits in the Senate committees proved a fairly futile exercise.

Another rather odd result of the new term limit for committee chairs was that House members who were now term limited as chair of one committee suddenly popped up as chair of another. By December 2000, Bob Stump (House Veterans' Affairs Committee), James Sensenbrenner (House Science Committee), Bill Thomas (House Oversight Committee) and Henry Hyde (House Judiciary Committee) had all completed their 6-year terms as committee chairs. But in January 2001, they merely reappeared as chairs of different committees — Stump now chaired Armed Services, Sensenbrenner now chaired Judiciary, Thomas now chaired Ways and Means, while Hyde turned up as chairman of the House International Relations Committee. It looked more like musical chairs than term limits.

Former Republican Congressman Vin Weber, a respected commentator on the institution and who in the mid-1990s supported term limits for committee chairs, now believes it was a big mistake. '[Republicans] who want to chair a committee are forced by internal politics to move to the right and in the case of Democrats to the left,' he said. Weber now believes this is another factor that increases polarisation in Congress

(4) Diffusion of power in Congress

Half a century ago, when presidents such as Dwight Eisenhower (1953–61), John F. Kennedy (1961–63) and Lyndon Johnson (1963–68) resided in the White House, Congress was run by a few powerful individuals — and they were all men. To get things done in Congress, all you needed was the agreement of this handful of powerful people — the Speaker, the Majority Leader and a few chairs of the most powerful committees. If they said something would be done, it was done. But nowadays, in the words of Professor Anthony King, 'the powerful few have become the considerably less powerful many'. Power has become much more diffused in Congress. Committee chairs have less autonomy. Sub-committee chairs have a bigger part of the action. Through the televised coverage of both chambers — since the 1970s — individual members

have become more visible and thus more influential. When a member of Congress appears live on C-SPAN or C-SPAN2, he becomes the focus of attention in a way that was unthinkable a few decades ago.

This diffusion of power has helped to make Congress a more open, accountable and democratic institution. You may therefore wonder why we are talking about this in a chapter entitled 'What's *wrong* with Congress?' But there is another side to this equation. Diffusion of power results in an institution that is more individualistic and therefore less cohesive. This less cohesive institution finds it more difficult to get things done — to get 218 votes in the House, or 51 votes in the Senate. Someone who worked in the Nixon White House in the early 1970s likened trying to piece together a successful vote in Congress to putting together small tiles in a great mosaic — a laborious, painstaking and time-consuming job.

The diffusion of power is another reason why Congress may be less productive than it ought to be, and why gridlock is not uncommon in Washington politics. The old way of doing things may have been somewhat undemocratic and autocratic, but at least the trains ran on time, so to speak.

(5) Ethical problems

In 2004, Lee Hamilton, a former Democrat House member from Indiana, published a book entitled *How Congress Works and Why You Should Care* (Indiana University Press). In Chapter 4, he addresses public criticisms of Congress and in so doing tells this story:

> Several years ago, I was watching the evening news on television when the anchorman announced the death of Wilbur Mills, the legendary former chairman of the House Ways and Means Committee. There was a lot he could have said. He might have recounted the central role Mills played in creating Medicare. Or he might have talked about how Mills helped shape the Social Security system and draft the tax code. But he didn't. Instead, he recalled how Mills's career had foundered after he had been found early one morning with an Argentinean stripper named Fanne Foxe. And then he moved on to the next story.

Hamilton's point is that the media tend to focus on scandals rather than achievements. He's right, of course. For every member of Congress who has embarrassed themselves and the institution itself by their unethical behaviour, there are tens — if not hundreds — of members going about their work in an honest and genuinely philanthropic way.

That said, Congress does seem to have had more than its fair share of scandal. When I typed 'Congress' and 'scandal' into Google, the response was 'about 2,910,000 results' in 0.09 seconds! Mark Foley, Tom DeLay, William Jefferson,

Gary Condit and James Traficant all come to mind, and that's just in the last few years. Gary Condit was a Republican congressman from California who served 7 terms in the House before losing a primary election in 2002, having been suspected of the murder of Chandra Levy, a young Washington intern. The case remains unresolved. James Traficant, a 7-term Democrat from Ohio, was expelled from the House in the same year after having been convicted of bribery, filing false tax returns and racketeering. He is currently serving an 8-year prison term. In June 2007, Democrat House member William Jefferson of Lousisana was indicted on charges of racketeering, money-laundering and bribery.

Then there were the institutional scandals — Abscam (1978), the House Bank scandal (1992) and the Jack Abramoff affair (2005), to name but three. Such scandals don't do much to reduce the scepticism that is so often associated with public service in US politics these days.

(6) 3-day working week

One of the changes that has occurred in Congress over the past two decades is the shape of the working week and, with it, the day-to-day lives of many members of Congress. Former Congressman Vin Weber recalled recently that when he was first elected to the House in 1980, Bill Frenzel — a fellow Republican from Wisconsin — advised him and other freshman Republicans to bring their families with them and make their home in or near Washington DC. 'He told us it was a great experience we'd want to share with our families,' remembers Weber. 'But it also encouraged friendships with people on the other side of the aisle. You'd see them at church, at a hockey game.' According to Weber, all that changed in the late 1980s, as more and more Americans came to view 'Washington politics' as bad. They criticised members for having a 'Beltway mentality'. (The Beltway is equivalent to London's M25: many members of Congress live 'inside the Beltway', hence they are said to have a 'Beltway mentality' — divorced from the rest of the country.) In contrast, when the Republicans won control of the House in November 1994, the newly elected House Speaker Newt Gingrich warned new Republican members not to relocate to Washington.

At around the same time, Congress introduced reforms to make it easier for members to spend more time at home in their state or district. The congressional working week was reorganised so that most of the debates and all the votes in both chambers occurred only between Tuesday morning and Thursday afternoon. Many members of Congress adopted a 3-day week in Washington and spent the remainder of the time back home. What was lost as a consequence was the social interaction that had taken place between differing members of

Congress, sometimes across party lines. Former Democrat House member David Skaggs of Colorado remembers how his wife made a personal friend of the wife of then Republican House member Bob Livingston. 'Laura Skaggs and Bonnie Livingston knew each other, so there was pressure on us to keep things friendly and respectful', remembers Skaggs, who deplores the fact that today's Washington politicians are 'losing the grounding in human family life.'

Even the much-criticised political junket was another opportunity for members of Congress from different parties to spend an extended period travelling and living with people who they wouldn't otherwise get to know. This helped to reinforce the civility of Congress, something which many observers see as on a sharp decline. All this is summed up by David Skaggs in the following way:

> The effect of [these changes] in the life of members of Congress has been pointed out — early to Washington, quickly home — and the compression of the work week, the increment in freneticism, the absence of any opportunity to get to know one's colleagues except in an adversarial setting… I think it's terribly important, and we've lost that grounding normal human life that reminds members, just like anybody else, of some other things beyond the battles of the workday.

(7) Senate's abuse of the filibuster

The filibuster in the Senate comes from every member's right of unlimited debate. It is an old Senate custom. But more recently it has been abused to frustrate the president's power to appoint judges to the federal courts. Between 1995 and 2001, Senate Republicans had used various tactics to frustrate Democrat president Bill Clinton's judicial appointments. In the three Congresses that met during this 6-year period, Clinton got only 69.5%, 80.0% and 62.1%, respectively, of his federal judicial nominations confirmed by the Republican-controlled Senate (see Table 6.3).

Table 6.3 Percentages of federal judges confirmed, 1995–2000

Years	Judges nominated	Judges confirmed	Percentage confirmed
1995–96	105	73	69.5
1997–98	125	100	80.0
1999–2000	116	72	62.1

But for the first time in 2003, the minority party in the Senate used the filibuster against judicial nominees that had already been given a recommendatory 'yes' vote by the Senate Judiciary Committee. It was this action by

Senate Democrats that caused President Bush to accuse the Senate of 'an abdication of constitutional responsibility.' That year, the Democrats effectively filibustered the nomination of four federal judges — Miguel Estrada, Priscilla Owen, William Pryor and Carolyn Kuhl — causing one of them (Estrada) to withdraw from the process. Estrada pulled out in September 2003 after Senate Republicans had failed on 7 separate occasions — spread over almost 5 months — to end the Democrats' filibuster tactics.

For their part, Senate Democrats shrugged off the criticism and accused President George W. Bush of trying to pack the federal courts with judges who were 'out of the mainstream' and of wanting the Senate to merely 'rubber stamp' his nominees in violation of their constitutional responsibility to scrutinise their qualifications.

In response to all this, then Senate Majority Leader, Republican Bill Frist, came up with a plan to change the Senate rules to make it no longer possible to filibuster judicial appointments, a plan which his fellow Republican Trent Lott dubbed 'the nuclear option'. But a number of senior Senate Republicans refused to back the idea.

Disaster on both sides was eventually averted by the formation of a bipartisan agreement between 14 Senators — 7 Democrats and 7 Republicans — to filibuster a judicial nomination only in 'extraordinary circumstances'. The 14 Senators who signed the agreement were mostly known for their moderate, centrist views — Republicans such as Lincoln Chafee, Susan Collins and John McCain, and Democrats such as Joseph Lieberman, Ben Nelson and Ken Salazar.

(8) Ineffective oversight of the executive branch

The Constitution does not specifically grant Congress the power of oversight of the executive branch. However, it does grant Congress law-making powers, and it is therefore implied that in order to make laws, Congress must find out how the current laws are operating. Hence the implied power of oversight of the executive branch, as it is the president who is charged with seeing that 'the laws be faithfully executed'.

Academics and commentators have often suggested that it is only when the executive and legislature are controlled by different parties — that is, under so-called divided government — that Congress's oversight of the executive branch is truly effective. The argument tends to go that when Congress and the White House are controlled by the same party, as was the case for the first 6 years of George W. Bush's presidency (with the 18-month exception of the Democrats' control of the Senate in 2001 and 2002), this congressional oversight is ineffective — Congress turns from being a watchdog to being a lapdog.

But there is also a danger that, even under divided government, congressional oversight of the executive branch may not be all that effective. In the last 6 years of his administration (1995–2001), President Clinton faced a Republican Congress. But the oversight conducted by the Republicans during this period too often looked more like personal attack and vindictiveness than effective scrutiny of the legislation, actions and nominations of the President. This climaxed in Congress's reaction to the Starr Report, impeachment and the trial of the President on counts of obstruction of justice and perjury.

As Brian Friel put it in a recent *National Journal* article ('The watchdog growls', 24 March 2007), the trouble is that 'what looks like well-intentioned good government oversight to one party might look like a partisan witch hunt to the other.' There's also the danger of tit-for-tat. Because the Democrats were upset at the Republicans going after President Clinton in the late 1990s, some of them wanted to go after President Bush when they took control of Congress in January 2007. According to Republican Senator Jim DeMint of South Carolina in March 2007, the Democrats' oversight of the Bush administration 'is a bunch of political posturing and demagoguery, and they haven't actually changed anything.' In other words, congressional oversight was still less than effective.

Conclusion

There is, therefore, plenty of evidence that Congress as an institution has a number of flaws. It is not rated highly by Americans. The paradox is that Americans regularly re-elect their Senators and House members. We have also revealed a number of specific things that are wrong with Congress. Is there anything that realistically can be done to correct any of these flaws?

The gerrymandering of House districts could be stopped by taking away the power to draw electoral boundaries from politicians and giving it, as in the UK, to independent bodies. The difficulty is that state legislatures are highly unlikely to vote this power away. Turkeys don't vote for an early Thanksgiving, so to speak. It is hard to see what can be done practically to lessen the levels of ideological polarisation. When the Democrats returned to power in Congress in January 2007 they did not continue the Republican-imposed rule about term limits for committee chairs. Some would argue that diffusion of power in Congress is more of a positive than a negative and ought not to be reversed. It does lead to Congress being a more accountable and democratic institution than used to be the case. Congress could certainly do itself a favour by putting in place more robust, and possibly independent, mechanisms for dealing with members who are accused of ethical misbehaviour. It might also be advantageous if Congress were to develop a working routine which encouraged members to spend rather more time in Washington. And both parties need to end the shenanigans over delaying the confirmation of appointments — especially judicial appointments — of which both have been guilty in the last decade and more. What would improve Congress's self-image more than anything, however, would be for ordinary Americans to feel that Congress was addressing their policy concerns in an imaginative and practical fashion and calling the executive branch to account, not out of spite, but in a genuine attempt to promote effective and accountable government. Are those pigs I see flying in the sky above Capitol Hill?

Task 6.1

Write a paragraph in which you analyse the statistics presented in Table 6.1 on congressional job ratings between 2001 and 2007.

Guidance

You will need to think about the political events that occurred during these years: the 9/11 attacks on the US (2001); foreign wars (2002); elections; change of party control (2007).

Task 6.2

Read the extract below from Jeffrey Toobin's 'The great election grab' (published in *The New Yorker*, 8 December 2003). Then answer the questions that follow.

Jeffrey Toobin on 'The great election grab'

Jim Leach, a moderate Republican Congressman from Iowa, has watched the transformation [to more and more safe House seats]. 'A district that is solidly Republican is a district that is more likely to go to the more conservative side of the Republican part of the Party for candidates and policies. If your House district is solidly one party, your only challenge is from within that party, so you have every incentive for staying to the more extreme side of your party. If you are a Republican in an all-Republican district, there is no reason to move to the centre. You want to protect your base. The American political system today is [therefore] structurally geared against the centre which means the great majority of Americans feel left out of the decision-making process.'

Scholarly research gives some support to Leach's impressions. 'Partisan gerry-mandering skews not only the positions congressmen take but also who the candidates are in the first place,' states Samuel Isaacharoff, a professor at Columbia Law School. 'You get more ideological candidates, the people who can

Task 6.2 (continued)

arouse the base of the party, because they don't have to worry about electability. With partisan gerrymandering, House members in effect pay a penalty if they reach out too much to members of the other party. [As a result] it's becoming harder to get things done in Congress.

(a) Explain why Jim Leach suggests that partisan gerrymandering results not only in more safe seats but also in more ideological politics.

(b) Explain how the research of Samuel Isaacharoff supports Jim Leach's views.

(c) Why do you think that, as a result of all this, Isaacharoff suggests that 'it's becoming harder to get things done in Congress'?

Guidance

(a) The clue is in Leach's comment about candidate selection.

(b) The key here is in Isaacharoff's comment about who gets selected in gerry-mandered districts.

(c) The conventional wisdom is that most things happen in Congress as a result of bipartisan cooperation and compromise. So why is this less likely to happen now, given what you have learnt from the comments of Leach and Isaacharoff?

Task 6.3

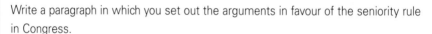

Write a paragraph in which you set out the arguments in favour of the seniority rule in Congress.

Guidance

These are set out on pp. 94–95. You might want to add some sentences about the arguments against the seniority rule.

Task 6.4

Read Sources A and B. Then answer the questions that follow.

Source A: '109th Congress gets props for creativity, if nothing else' by Dana Milbank (*Washington Post*, 28 September 2006)

There are just a couple of days left in the life of the 109th Congress (2005–06) and lawmakers are getting a bit punch-drunk. Congress has yet to agree on a single one of its 12 annual spending bills, but the House managed to find time yesterday to consider H. Res. 748, 'Recognising the 225th Anniversary of the American and French victory at Yorktown.' Congress still hasn't worked out immigration legislation

Task 6.4 (continued)

or lobbying reform, but the House yesterday moved to embrace H. Res. 991, 'Congratulating the Columbus Northern Little League Baseball Team from Columbus, Georgia.' There's nothing doing on port security or Social Security, but there was broad agreement yesterday on H. Res. 973, honouring 'the financial planning profession for their adherence and dedication to the financial planning process.'

Measured by days in session or legislative output, this Congress has secured its place as one of the most lethargic of all time. But if historians choose to award points for creativity, the 109th could go down in the books as a most prolific body.

Consider Rep. David Dreier (R-California), the dapper chairman of the House Rules Committee. On Tuesday, his committee ruled that the House would not consider some 15 amendments the Democrats had proposed to legislation on military commissions. Then, on the House floor yesterday, Dreier scolded the Democrats for not offering an alternative.

Or consider Senate Majority Leader Bill Frist (R-Tennessee), who, in front of the microphones yesterday, quarrelled with the Democrats' characterisation of this as a 'do-nothing Congress'. Asked for tangible achievements, Frist responded with a 650-word answer that listed only two items that had cleared Congress: the confirmation of Supreme Court Justice Samuel Alito and Chief Justice John Roberts.

Source B: 'Do-Nothing Congress vilified' by Christina Bellantoni (*Washington Times*, 6 September 2006)

Democrats seeking to return to power [in Congress] have labelled the House of Representatives the 'Do-Nothing Congress'. The legislative calendar as it stands today includes fewer than 20 working days before members break to campaign for the November 7 elections. Democrats point out the House will have worked just 84 days this year unless the schedule is altered. The 80th Congress spent 108 days in session in 1948 when President Truman famously labelled it the 'Do-Nothing Congress' for his re-election campaign.

(a) What evidence does Dana Milbank produce for Congress's failure to address the major policy concerns of many Americans?

(b) Why does Milbank suggest that the 109th Congress was 'one of the most lethargic of all time'? What further evidence is there for this in Source B?

(c) Who invented the phrase the 'Do-Nothing Congress'? When was this phrase first popularised?

(d) What do the examples of David Dreier and Bill Frist show about what's wrong with Congress?

Task 6.4 (continued)

Guidance

(a) The key is in what the 109th Congress was *not* addressing as opposed to what it had spent its time actually doing in these last few days of Congress.

(b) The word 'lethargic' means 'lazy' or 'inactive'.

(c) The answer is in Source B. You could find out more about this by visiting the on-line encyclopaedia **www.wikipedia.org**.

(d) Think about why ordinary Americans would criticise the actions of David Dreier or the claims of Bill Frist.

Further reading

- Brady, D. and Volden, C. (2006) *Revolving Gridlock*, Westview.
- Hamilton, L. (2004) *How Congress Works*, Indiana University Press.
- Mann, T. and Ornstein, N. (2006) *The Broken Branch: How Congress is Failing America*, Oxford University Press.